Candid Classroom

Erica Ladd

Interior Design by: Darrell Vesterfelt of Nashville, Tennessee
Cover Design by: Thoughtful Revolution of Austin, Texas
Author Photograph by: Gretchen Wakeman
Editing by: Allison Vesterfelt

ISBN-13: 978-0-989702-02-7

DEDICATION

To my first class of 17 little ones at Vernon Elementary who made me a teacher for the very first time.

I will always cherish the title, "Maestra."

CONTENTS

FOREWORD: *WHAT HAPPENS WHEN WE LISTEN*

Before I was a writer, I was a teacher for a few years and, in those few years, I decided teaching is the second hardest job on the planet. The first hardest job on the planet is being a parent. What's interesting is parents and teachers have an awful lot in common. They both want what's best for their kids (however "their" kids are defined), they both will go to great lengths to do what's best for their kids, and they each find themselves, at times, confused about what the "best" truly is.

We're both—teachers and parents, alike—asking this question: What's best for our kids and how can we give it to them?

As we work to discover the answer to this question, we might disagree at times. We might change our minds. We might land on various strong opinions. But here's the truly crazy thing about the task of parents and teachers: If parents and teachers could find a way to communicate with one another, their job would be so much simpler.

There is so much wisdom to share. There is so much learning

to be done. So much of who your child is remains unknown to his or her teacher; and so much of what happens during the day, while your child is at school, remains unknown to you. We could be great allies, parents and teachers. And yet, somehow, this never seems to happen.

When I was teaching, one particular student tugged at my heartstrings. The story of my time with him demonstrates this example perfectly and, to this day, he remains one of my most memorable students. His name was Ahmed.

I didn't know much about Ahmed when he first came to me. I knew he was an eighth grader, and that he had recently moved with his family from Rwanda. I knew his spoken English was proficient, but if he didn't catch up with his reading and writing he was in danger of not moving on to high school. Over time I learned a few more things about him—that he loved basketball and couldn't sit still for more than two minutes at a time. I learned he had a boisterous personality, and was never afraid to say what was on his mind. I learned he had an opinion about everything.

And although I started my teaching career with all kinds of ideals about being a teacher who didn't marginalize kids or judge them, who always expected the best out of them and called them to their highest selves, when it came time to put those ideas into practice, with Ahmed, I found it more difficult than I expected.

I found myself saying the same things to Ahmed, over and over again. "Ahmed, why are you out of your seat?" "Ahmed, where's your backpack?" "Ahmed, are you even listening to me?"

Before long I had resigned to the assumption that Ahmed could never, and probably would never, learn to read and write well enough to move on to high school. I wished I could do something to help him, but I figured I had already done everything I could.

Then one day while I was in the middle of a thrilling lecture about the correct use of exclamation points, Ahmed interrupted me, mid-sentence.

"Why's you so lonely, miss?"

"Excuse me?" I asked.

"You's so lonely all the time. How come?"

I stood shocked on my little teacher's pedestal at the front of the room and, without a word, continued the lecture, but Ahmed wasn't fazed. He raised his hand, as I had instructed him (numerous times) to do when he had a question.

"Do you have a question, Ahmed?" I asked.

"Yes, Ma'am."

"Is it about exclamation points?"

"No Ma'am." (At least he was honest).

I asked him to wait until after class, assuming that would deter him. But it didn't. In fact, after class he came to my desk, even more intense than before.

"Why's you so lonely, Miss?" He asked, looking across my desk. I shuffled papers back and forth as I talked, trying to explain how I didn't know what he was talking about. Eventually, at my insistence, he meandered to his next class, leaving me alone for the next forty-five minutes—my prep period.

As soon as the door shut behind him, I cried.

I cried because he was right and I couldn't figure out how he noticed. I cried because, as far as I could tell, I had convinced everyone else I wasn't lonely and this kid was the only one who had figured me out.

A few months later, during parent-teacher conferences, I learned there was more to Ahmed than just a larger-than-life personality and a love for basketball. I learned his parents had been killed in the Rwandan genocide and his aunt and uncle had fled to the United States and brought him with them. I learned his uncle was a well-meaning, hard-working man who was now acting as his father, and who barely spoke English. I learned that a lot was expected of Ahmed—he was in charge of taking care of several younger siblings and his uncle raised his voice to Ahmed when he discovered he wasn't getting better grades.

I watched tears well up in Ahmed's eyes, feelings of failure overwhelming him. This sweet twelve-year-old kid tried to hold it together but it was no use. While I watched him fight back tears of loss and pain, I thought of the day he told me I was lonely. He saw me that day and, now, I saw him too.

I talked with Ahmed's uncle and we made a plan together. We agreed on a certain place Ahmed would sit in the classroom, and that Ahmed would be allowed to stay after school for the homework program to get extra help. We agreed he would bring his backpack to school every day, with pencils and paper in it, so he could do his work. We agreed, all three of us together, that no matter what, Ahmed was going to make it to high school.

After that, things changed with me and Ahmed. Where I used to think I had "done everything I could," I started to see more ways I could help. I would stay late, come early, soften my tone and even lie awake at night wondering what else I could do to be a better teacher to him. I started to understand Ahmed better, and I couldn't have done it without his uncle's help.

Something powerful happens when we listen to each other. Not "listen" in the superficial sense of the word, but really listen—for something other than our own agenda, for the sake of someone else. Suddenly we begin to see things we had missed before. Things become clearer. Everything starts to look up.

To me, this book is the start of something beautiful because it's the start of a conversation like that. This is a chance to listen—to listen to things you didn't previously know or understand about your child, from a teacher's perspective; to begin to see things more clearly and for everything to start looking up. It's not the end-all-be-all. It's not the final word on school or your child. It's not the "Gospel" of what they should wear or how they should act. It's actually something better. It's a smart, talented, experienced, honest perspective about your child and what really happens all day in their classroom.

And if you listen—really listen—things just might start to shift...

Allison Vesterfelt, author of Packing Light

INTRODUCTION

I slump down at the horseshoe-shaped table, clearing away the project Kaitlyn didn't finish and the stack of baseball cards I confiscated from Trevor to make room for my lunch. I hastily wipe the surface with an antibacterial wipe, because goodness knows what germs remain from reading groups. My fellow second grade teachers straggle in with their lunches, various caffeinated beverages, and stacks of spelling tests to grade as they shovel food into their mouths. We've all deposited our students in the cafeteria, leaving us exactly thirty minutes to eat and compose ourselves before Round Two. We've made it to the halfway point in the day and school year, and we look it.

As we unpack our lunches with sighs of exhaustion, we recount funny stories and rewarding moments, alongside frustrations over inherent difficulties of the occupation. One teacher will need to jet in a minute to get an activity together for a parent volunteer who is coming in spontaneously to help that afternoon. I am nervous for a parent meeting after school with a mother who wants to discuss everything from seating arrangements to homework accommodations, which promises to make for an 11-hour day for me once again. Another teacher wolfs down her food, because she needs to go answer an email from an upset parent who is convinced his son is being bullied on the playground and nothing is being done about it. A common theme that emerges in conversation is that parents and teachers are often just not on the same page.

Teachers are trying their best to juggle the educational needs of a classroom full of students. Sometimes, parents just want to know whether or not their child is eating enough at lunch, or how they are doing socially. They wonder if any other dads are having difficulty remembering second grade math, or if they're a bad mom for skipping the bedtime story last night. They've heard great things about this teacher and awful things about that one, but aren't sure what to believe as they wonder whose class their child will end up in next year. They get frustrated with a lack of communication from their child's teacher about their progress, but wonder if maybe no news is good news. They just want to be involved and supportive, but are not quite sure how.

I can't help but notice something wrong here. Why does there seem to be this unnecessary disconnect between school and home? Why such a huge gap between what's actually going on in schools, and what parents think or expect is going on in schools? Why does it seem teachers and parents are often not even talking about the same child when discussing a student? Something is missing. I feel we've failed, somehow as teachers, to represent ourselves and what happens in the classroom accurately. We've lost the truth and the ability to see each other as a community somewhere in the exhaustion and politics of education. I think an honest conversation would start to change that.

Parenting and teaching are both crazy hard. Why do we spend so much time and energy pretending they're not? It so often feels we are barely keeping our heads above water, so we hide away. Parents make assumptions or avoid directly asking a teacher a question, because they don't want to admit they don't have it all figured out. Teachers too often hide behind time restraints, and use educational buzz words to put up a wall in the name of professionalism. The truth of the matter is, we're afraid to have a frank discussion with each other about what matters most, the students. Teachers assume parents should be understanding and involved and become frustrated when they are not. If we want them to really get it—to know what it's like at school, and how to best support their child, then why don't we just tell them?

I have been an elementary teacher for over eight years, and have always felt school should come with a guide book for parents. So, I've created one. This book is filled with a behind-the-scenes look at the world behind the classroom door. I want to give parents an honest, often humorous, peek at those things that are not typically covered during parent-teacher conferences. This book is about what teachers desperately want to sit down and discuss with parents over coffee, the things we tell our own sisters and friends as they send their little ones off to kindergarten. It will cover everything from homework and volunteering in the classroom, to bathroom breaks and bullying.

Parents are their child's first and most important teachers. Nothing is more valuable than the parent/child relationship for development and future success. Children learn early on from parents as they watch their ways, listen to their language, and mimic their actions. Then enters the teacher, and the child takes on a new role. They are no longer just a son or daughter, but they become a student. This new parent/student/teacher relationship is a complicated dance of educating young minds together, and sometimes parents are left wondering how it's supposed to work.

I can point to ample research about parental involvement and its effect on a child's academic success. Statistics abound, correlating the number of minutes per day spent reading with a child to their future literacy. But I think what's often ignored in these numbers is the story. The statistics and the research go in one ear and out the other. I can give you a handout at Open House about those things, but what we have not done a great job of as teachers, is to sit down and tell you some stories.

As a parent, you have trusted teachers with your greatest treasure, and we should hold it with open hands, letting you see into the world of the classroom, and walk a day in our shoes. I want to tell you what really concerns us as teachers, what really matters, and what parents and teachers can do about it together. I want to tell you the funny stories, the impossible situations, and the beautiful moments happening with your children every day.

This book will not give you a magic formula to guarantee your child's entrance to Harvard, or tell you which cereal to buy to ensure higher test scores. What it will do is answer some questions I have been most often asked as a teacher, and hopefully alleviate some fears of that teary-eyed mom at the bus stop on the first day of school. I want to put the politics and the barriers aside. We will step away from test scores and report cards, teacher lingo and mommy guilt, and take a real look inside the classroom, where teachers are given the extraordinary privilege of helping parents educate their children.

CHAPTER ONE: *BUTT CRACKS, KINDERGARTEN, AND HOW TO REALLY PREPARE YOUR CHILD FOR SCHOOL*

She kissed Mommy goodbye, and skipped down the front steps. Mommy had decided it might go better if Papi took over this particular task. She gripped Papi's hand as they walked the two blocks to school for the first day of kindergarten. As the red brick building grew closer, they turned the last corner, and her grip tightened with sweaty palms.

The night before, they had dropped off her school supplies in a brown grocery bag as she met her teacher and shyly looked around her new classroom. Mommy excitedly pointed out the play area and her name at her seat as she hesitantly took it all in. Now this morning, it was taking all of her courage under her tight bun and new first-day outfit to walk to school for the first time.

When they got to the kindergarten meeting spot on the playground, she watched with big brown eyes as some kids clung to their moms, who all seemed to be wearing sunglasses. One big boy was even crying, but she felt brave as she took deep breaths like Mommy had taught her to calm her nerves, shuffling her feet and kicking at rocks with her shiny school shoes.

After school that day, everyone seemed so excited to hear all about her first day of kindergarten. "How was your day?!" Mommy sang as she picked her up.

"Fine," she said.

"What'd you learn about?" Mommy asked.

"I don't remember," she replied matter-of-factly.

Her formerly neat bun was now a hot sweaty mess of hair. Her shirt was untucked and her pleated khaki skirt askew. When she got home she devoured a snack of cheese and crackers while staring with glazed eyes toward her cartoons. After a bit, she crawled into Papi's lap with her blanket and slept right through dinner with her two middle fingers in her mouth, a sweet reminder she was still their little girl after a very big day.

This was my niece Anahi's first day of kindergarten. About seven years ago, the string of nieces began for us. Between my brother, sister, and brother-in-law there were three nieces all born within that year. This means they all started talking around the same time, got potty trained around the same time, and of course all started kindergarten the same fall. It's been so fun watching them go through big milestones together, and I can hardly believe that they are all in school now.

As a former kindergarten teacher I was so excited for them to start, knowing how much they would grow that first year of elementary school. Kindergarten was by far my favorite age to teach. There is absolute magic when kids start to make the connection between those ABC's they've been singing since they were two, and the written word. They start to read stories and write their own as confidence grows. There is nothing like watching the whole world of literacy open up to a little one, and it is such a privilege to be a part of it!

I've always been the one on the other side of the classroom door, but talking to my sister those first days of kindergarten, about what it was like from her perspective to hand over her baby, got me thinking. I had never really focused on just how hard that must be for parents. August and September are filled with anxiety for families across the country, and I know there are uncertain tears, more from the mamas than their kids. I don't really know what that feels like yet, but I have decided to help you out with what I do know.

So, to all the moms and dads who dropped off their pride and joy at those classroom doors for the first time, and then went home and ugly cried, there are some things your child's kindergarten teacher was too tired to tell you at the end of the first day or even week, but would probably like you to know. . .

School Is Exhausting

Your child is going to be completely exhausted for a while (as is their teacher). It is a long day for little bodies (and big ones). Be patient and allow time for everyone, (including yourself), to develop a rhythm. A new routine of packing lunches, checking backpacks and folders, waking up early, homework, and after school activities can really turn the household upside down.

Develop a system that works for you with designated places for all of the new things school brings, and it will make life easier. You may feel like you don't know what to do with the endless stream of papers, permission slips and art projects, or how your front hall suddenly became so cluttered with lunch boxes, backpacks, and bike helmets. Here's the thing: the sooner you can establish routines and procedures for where those things go, the sooner they can become your child's responsibility, taking up less energy and room in your brain. (We'll this idea of encouraging independence and responsibility further in Chapter 2.)

Your child might be just plain wiped out for the first few weeks and maybe even months of school. It is a long day for them, and they may need a nap when they get home. If they are cranky and exhausted every afternoon or evening after around the halfway point in the school year, it may be a sign they need to go to bed earlier. Kids need lots of sleep when their little brains and bodies are busy throughout the day growing and stretching in new ways, and sometimes we don't realize they aren't really getting enough.

Plus, an earlier bedtime for them means more grown-up time for you.

You also may notice an increase in your child's appetite after starting school. They are expending a lot of energy throughout the day, and growing brains need fuel. Besides, a cafeteria full of 100 or more kids can be a distracting place at first, so they often don't eat all of their lunch. Soon, they will adjust, and will probably start finishing their lunch more consistently. In the beginning, just know they have a lot to take in at lunchtime, and it can be overwhelming initially. Not to worry, it will soon be their new normal, but in the meantime you can help by making sure they are eating a healthy breakfast (yogurt and a banana as you fly out the door totally count), and filling snacks.

Your kids are likely adjusting to a new sleeping and eating routine, and it may just take their body a bit to fully adapt. Snacks and meals are scheduled at school, and those may not be the times they are used to eating. In addition, they are probably going to bed and getting up earlier than they are used to. Soon, things will work themselves out.

Along those lines, we teachers may look all put together the first week or so of school. We may even wear heels or a tie because the school year is still shiny and new, but just know that we too are exhausted. I promise, even the most seasoned teacher needs a week or two to get into a routine as he or she is getting to know the students.

In kindergarten especially, it is physically taxing just to make sure all those little bodies stay together and everyone makes it back from a bathroom break. On top of that, teachers have spent countless hours setting up their classroom, rearranging, and reorganizing. So, you may need to cut him or her some slack in returning phone calls or emails at first. If they seem a little scattered on the playground at pick-up time, they probably are, but don't write them off as a flake just yet. They are juggling a lot! Give them the benefit of the doubt, and maybe bring them an iced coffee or a Diet Coke. August and September are hot, and caffeine is always appreciated.

Dress for Success

Children can be whirlwinds of activity, and the state of their clothing at the end of the day reflects that. Think of the last time you spent a full day with your child—just a typical day, with breakfast, maybe an errand or two, playing in the backyard for a bit, maybe some play dough, lunch, a nap, a snack. Now picture your child at the end of the day. What does their hair look like? Are there dirt smudges and scraped knees? Are there holes in their jeans and sand in their shoes? Most likely.

Now consider their day at school. They are playing on the playground several times throughout the day in all kinds of weather. They are eating and spilling snack, lunch, and possibly even breakfast with other kindergarteners who may or may not spill their respective snacks, lunches, and possible breakfasts on your child as well. In addition to playing and eating, they are sitting, dancing, building, coloring, painting, gluing, and cutting daily. Kindergarten is a messy business, so please dress your child for the day they will actually have.

Allow me to break it down in the clothing department for a moment. I have promised practical advice, and practical advice is what you shall receive. There are important things to consider while helping your child get dressed for school. For starters, the home base of learning in kindergarten, and really for all of early elementary school, likely takes place on a brightly colored carpet. This means little bottoms sitting with legs crossed on the floor for a good portion of their day. Please remember this when you are helping your child don their adorable skirt, or their trendy jeans in the morning. Since little ones have not exactly mastered the art of propriety, and apparently are also unaffected by drafts, I would recommend what I like to call a tooshie test. Have your little one sit down and stand up multiple times in succession. If there is any sign of tooshie, might I suggest an outfit change? You do not want your kid to be the one with a perpetually visible butt crack. How's that for something they won't tell you on Meet the Teacher Night?

Now for some real talk about footwear choices: First of all, I need you to know children will play hard in whatever kind of shoes they are wearing. While they may keep their patent leather Sunday best shoes pristine under your watchful eye, all bets are off at school. Peer pressure will force them to actually play on the playground, so just know those shoes may come home from school looking less than shiny.

Can we discuss flip-flops? As an adult, I don't know that I've ever broken a flip-flop. I generally wear them for lounging next to the pool or wandering through a store on a hot day. Children do not do the same things in flip-flops that adults do. They run at maximum speed and blow out flip-flops more frequently than tires at the Indy 500. So, if I were helping my child pick out sandals for school, they would involve ankle straps and nice sturdy bottoms. Avoid flip flops.

While we're on the subject, shoelaces also present unique educational challenges. Let me paint you a picture of what it's like to have a classroom full of five year olds who don't know how to tie their shoes. It looks like me bent over, with possible aforementioned butt crack showing, tying shoes all day which have been dragged through sand, and puddles of rain, mud, slush, snow, and bathroom. This is unsanitary, bad for my back, and quite frankly, it's very difficult to teach from this position.

As a result, tying shoes became a job I delegated in my classroom. When students learned to tie their shoes, they received an award and were deemed the official shoe helpers of the classroom. Some students, of course, came to school already knowing how to tie their shoes. So when I introduced the board, their name went up right away. When other students needed a shoe tied, they were to find a shoe helper. You should see the pride in the smirk of a little one as they puff out their chest, hike up their pants, and stoop down to tie a classmate's shoe for them. The moral of the story is: when in doubt, choose velcro, unless of course your child has high hopes of being a shoe helper, in which case some practice at home will be necessary.

Another thing to keep in mind is, even at school, accidents happen. This is especially true during the first few weeks of school when students are figuring out where the bathroom is, how to ask to go to the bathroom, or prying themselves away from an exciting activity long enough to actually use the bathroom. Waiting until the last minute and sprinting to the bathroom is commonplace. A change of clothes in your child's backpack will save them an uncomfortable wait in the nurse's office while you leave work to bring them dry underwear.

To sum up, dress your child realistically for an active day, please teach them to tie their shoes, and always make sure they have a change of clothes at the ready.

Change is Hard for Everybody

If on that first day of school your child cried a little, (or screamed, clung to you and had to be physically peeled away by the teacher), they were much better after you left, I promise. They always are. And it gets easier as they become more familiar with their new surroundings. The unknown is scary for all of us, but it should feel good that you are their safe place.

That being said, you need to show them with your actions that school is a safe place as well. When you confidently and matter-of-factly drop them off with a kiss and a hug into the capable hands of their teacher, you are communicating with them they are taken care of and will be just fine. They might need to borrow your confidence at first, and you may need to fake it a bit until you too are more confident letting go. It's a good practice for everyone involved. Raising kids is about preparing them and then letting go one step at a time throughout their lives, so it's important.

When children are feeling a little anxious, you would be amazed at how parents hovering around the classroom can actually exacerbate the problem. When you do that as a parent, you are communicating to your child they need you to be safe. They may sense you don't quite trust them to be independent, or their teachers to take good care of them.

You're also depriving them of an opportunity to learn how to deal with fear and anxiety in healthy ways. All of us have fears, but we need to learn how to push through and not be paralyzed by them. That's how we grow in confidence, and for your little one it may be one of their first chances to feel some fear and do it anyway. Isn't that the kind of adult we want our children to become—the confident kind who aren't afraid to take risks and see rewards, proud of themselves at the end of the day?

From a logistical standpoint, it is also difficult to wrangle 30 kindergarteners into a routine, especially when their parents are hovering by the coat rack. Kids thrive on routine and procedures, and I can guarantee they will settle into them quickly and comfortably if they are allowed to do so.

I can also guarantee your child learned something on any given day, even if they told you they didn't. Children at this age learn mostly through play. If learning is presented in a fun and natural way, they may not think of it as learning at all. One of my favorite responses from a five-year-old when asked where they learned something is "from my brain." They assume they've always known it, and are often not yet reflective about their own learning.

Something else you may notice is students are also starting to develop their "school self" and often want it kept separate from their "home self." It may be their first attempt at creating their own identity away from home, and sometimes they don't like mixing those two worlds. Remember that feeling as a kid when you brought your parents to open house, feeling weird and a little embarrassed to have them looking inside your desk, talking to your friends, and touching your artwork in the hallway? Or do you recall running into your teacher at the grocery store and feeling suddenly mortified your two worlds were colliding right there in the produce department? It's like that.

Four Things Your Child Needs Before Kindergarten

As a parent, you have probably done so much to prepare your little one for school without even realizing it. Whole books are written on the subject of what to do to prepare your child for kindergarten, but it really boils down to four things in my opinion.

Some of my colleagues may disagree with me about how prepared a student needs to be before entering kindergarten. But while things like writing their name, knowing their letters and sounds, and number recognition are nice, the truth of the matter is there are four things which are truly essential. If you've ever colored pictures, sang songs, read books, or said no to your child, they are ready. In my experience those four things alone can easily provide the foundation a child needs to be successful their first year of school. Allow me to elaborate.

Coloring pictures is about so much more than entertaining your child at a restaurant while they wait for their food. Think of all the essential skills going on while coloring. It's fine motor development as they learn to grasp a writing utensil and control it to make purposeful marks on a page. Hello emergent writer! There's also color recognition, and decision making taking place. They are learning how to follow through on a task until it's completed. Also, they're likely talking to someone about what they are drawing or coloring, and in doing so, building their vocabulary and conversation skills. Most importantly they are creating something. Kids are learning they are capable of making something from nothing, adding color where there was none, and beginning to take pride in their work.

In addition to coloring together, every time you sing a song, or even expose your child to music on the radio or television, you are also developing something very important to your child's future literacy. It's called phonemic awareness, which is a fancy way of saying "an awareness of sounds." Think about why this is important for a minute. When we read or write, we are reading or writing language. Language is made up of words, which are made up of sounds. The rhyme, repetition, and rhythm of language are reinforced in songs. It's why we sing nursery rhymes with little ones, and why even just sitting that little bottom in front of Sesame Street can be so beneficial.

Similarly, when you read a book with your child, you are laying another important foundation for their future literacy. It doesn't matter how long the book is, what language it's in, or how many times you've read it before. They see you turning pages, reading from left to right, and connecting meaning to the pictures and words on the page. You are modeling reading in as natural of a thing as a bedtime story or a quick tale in the waiting room at the doctor's office.

Finally, every time you have said no to your child, set an expectation, or followed through on a consequence, you have taught them there are expectations in life. You are setting them up to be able to understand the limits in a formal educational setting. Imagine how valuable this lesson will be in the classroom when they understand you don't just get up and leave the classroom whenever you feel like it, or decide you're going to color a picture instead of sitting on the carpet and listening to a story.

In my opinion, the rest of the academics are my job as a teacher, and if you've provided them with those four things, it makes that job a lot easier. Now certainly, the more you can work on other basic skills—like letters, numbers, and counting—the more familiar those concepts will be for your child. It is never a bad thing to get more practice at home, and as we progress through the year, a good teacher will give you all sorts of other ideas about specific skills they might need to work on at home and how to practice them.

But stop and take some pressure off of yourself for a moment. Before they ever walk through my door, you have taught them so much, and if you were expected as a parent to teach them everything before they ever even got to me, then what would be my purpose as a teacher? They are ready. Every time you colored with them, sang songs, read books, and followed through on a consequence, you helped them develop essential skills to be successful in school.

You Know Your Child Best

That being said, there is another side to the readiness coin. Some kids are actually just not quite ready yet, but in my experience, it has nothing to do with academics. It is usually a matter of emotional maturity and attention span. You know your child best, and only you can truly decide if they are ready to start school. Unfortunately in education, we seem to be pushing kids to start things earlier and earlier, but developmentally, some kids just aren't ready, and that's OK.

If your child has a late birthday for example, and turns five just before the cutoff to start kindergarten, look at it honestly to determine if they are truly ready. When in doubt, I tend to err on the side of waiting another year. Time is a gift for some kids, allowing them to start school confidently from the beginning—instead of struggling to make it through a day without crying, or sit still for more than two minutes at a time. It is a frustrating year for students, teachers, and parents when a child is constantly operating at a disadvantage in terms of maturity and ability to handle the emotional challenges of school. You know your child best. Trust your instincts on whether they are ready or not.

Overall, remember you are still your child's first and most important teacher. You know them best. Don't ever forget that or underestimate the impact you have on their everyday life.

"Dropping off your little one is tough, but we will take care of them as if they were our own."

Jill Traxler, Special Education Teacher

"Kindergarten is a year of exciting and explosive growth. From learning how to pump your legs on the swing, to differentiating between capital and lowercase letters, kindergarten is the year where cultivating a love for school and learning is taking place."

Amy Denny, Kindergarten Teacher

CHAPTER TWO: *HELICOPTERS, INDEPENDENCE, AND WHY YOU SHOULD STOP CARRYING YOUR CHILD'S BACKPACK*

I pulled into the school parking lot late one morning with only 15 minutes to spare before the first bell rang. Students were already starting to arrive on the playground as I screeched into my usual spot and threw the car in park. I looked up to see a family walking down the sidewalk on their way to school. The boy, who I recognized as a first grader, skipped, carefree and empty handed, ahead of his mom who was pushing a baby in a stroller. She trudged hurriedly behind him with a weary mix of "I hope these yoga pants don't have a hole in them" and "why does school start so early?" written all over her face.

The six-year-old obliviously attacked invisible enemies with an equally invisible sword half a block in front of his mother. Meanwhile, I noticed his mom was steering the stroller with one hand, with his Disney Cars backpack thrown over one of her hunched shoulders, and what I can only assume was his recently abandoned scooter slung over the other one. I forgot my current rushed state and my own rough morning for a moment to simply stare in awe with a dropped jaw.

To be clear, I was not staring at her misfortune or the difficult time she was obviously having. I was not having the most successful of mornings either with only myself to get ready, so I was in no place to judge. I don't know the exact story of this mother's morning. At home, there may have been kicking and screaming and refusing to put pants on by one or both of her children. There could have been slamming of doors, spilling of milk, and gnashing of teeth, all before leaving the house. What I couldn't believe was how hard she was making it on herself.

I know it's not easy, but I so badly wanted to help her to see there is a less difficult way. I know her seven year old is indeed capable of riding his own scooter while wearing his own backpack. I know the already stressful, demanding job of mothering two children at that early hour becomes much more so when they are not expected to take responsibility for themselves and their own things in age appropriate ways. In my experience, children need and often want to be independent and responsible, and it is our job as adults to teach them how to do so, and then expect them to.

The Problem with Doing It for Them

To a mom or dad who is accustomed to schlepping diaper bags, strollers, groceries, and various childhood supplies since taking on the role of parent, this may just seem like part of the deal. "I'm a parent, therefore I schlep," you think to yourself, "and I take care of things because nobody else will." When your child is an infant, of course you will need to haul and keep track of everything for them. But before they can even speak in complete sentences, children can be taught to, and in fact enjoy, cleaning up after themselves and being responsible for their own things. The key is making it commonplace from the very beginning.

My friend Jenny is an excellent example of this. One morning, I watched her 18-month-old daughter, Parker, while Jenny went to work. Parker and I had a full morning, complete with crackers, juice, and much destruction of the playroom.

When Jenny returned home, she joined us in the playroom for a bit. I was so impressed when she then guided Parker to put every last toy back where it belonged before it was time to move on to lunch. And you know what? She did! At 18-months-old, she knew exactly what to do. There was no power struggle or tantrum, because it was simply the routine. Now, Jenny definitely assisted her in putting things away, but she didn't do it all for her, which communicated a very important message: these were Parker's toys, and therefore ultimately Parker's responsibility. Besides saving Jenny from keeping the house in order all by herself down the road, she is also showing Parker she is a capable and helpful little person.

Some of the common behavior seen during the "terrible twos" stems from the fact that children want and are able to do so much more than we often allow them to. They are fiercely independent at this stage, and crave opportunities to show us what they can do. By showing Parker how to clean up her own toys, expecting her to do so, and then applauding her for a job well done, Jenny is teaching her that she can and should be responsible for her own things. Parker is growing in confidence and responsibility every day as a result.

You may be thinking to yourself, "Yeah right! That's a nice theory, but you have never met my 18-month-old, or her five-year-old and seven-year-old sibling, who assist her in wreaking havoc upon the entire household." It is certainly true that no two children are exactly the same.

But, as a classroom teacher, I have to tell you, your kids sometimes have you fooled. Many of them have you carrying their backpacks, cleaning their rooms, and even finishing their homework for them to avoid an emotional meltdown or save time. Being in the classroom with tiny scholars all day, I am witness to the fact they can do so much more than you might think.

I saw a perfect example of this in college when I worked part time at a fantastic corporate child care. A big focus of the school was meal time with the little ones. Teachers and staff even had their meals included as a part of their compensation, and there was a strict grandmotherly figure cooking breakfast and lunch every day. (Seriously, to this day, the best biscuits I've ever tasted came from that day care kitchen.) Teachers and assistants were expected to eat with the kids, and lots of learning was centered around eating family style, fostering conversation and independence.

I was shocked the first time I worked in the two-year-old room and saw kids who were not even potty-trained serving themselves out of a bowl of green beans and pouring their own milk into tiny real glasses with child-sized pitchers. Sure they spilled occasionally and needed help at times, but the point was for them to learn to do it on their own. There were so many less tantrums over the food on a child's plate when they had put it there themselves.

The experience stuck with me, and I have brought those high expectations for student independence into my own classroom. Your kiddos might be working the system at home, because at school they are going about their day with all kinds of independence and responsibility. They are expected to follow directions, clean up after themselves, and solve problems, and so they do, because it's essential to the day not disintegrating into complete chaos.

Imagine how ridiculous it would be if every student I taught came into the classroom and whipped their backpack on the floor or at me, expecting me to put it away. What if they didn't have a designated place to hang them up every morning, and just flung them around the classroom wherever they pleased as they came in to start the day? What if every day ended with all of them

25

frantically searching for their things and yelling for me to help them? This of course seems silly and out of the question, because nothing would ever get done in the classroom, and the students would never learn any independence. We wouldn't dream of our kids behaving that way at school, so why do we let them do it at home? You'd be amazed at what they can do! So, don't let them dupe you into thinking they are incapable of independence and responsibility.

Another problem with your children becoming accustomed to you doing everything for them is the level of disrespect that is often tolerated. It is a pet peeve of mine when a fully capable, energetic young boy heaves his backpack at his mom during after school pick-up and she dutifully picks it up and carries it without so much as a "please" or "thank you" from her son. How on Earth are we going to raise young people who offer to help an elderly lady to her car with groceries, or to lift a heavy bag into an overhead compartment on a plane for someone who's struggling, if they're allowed to treat their mom as a personal pack animal? If we ever expect our sons and daughters to willingly bear another's burdens out of compassion and respect, we might want to start with expecting them to bear their own backpack.

Besides the missed opportunities for independence and disrespectful behavior, doing everything for your children is just plain exhausting. Parenting is hard work. It is a physically, emotionally, and mentally draining job. These little humans are depending on you for all kinds of needs to be met, so why not allow them to meet the ones they can on their own?

It is not selfish to admit you cannot do everything on your own. There is no need to. Take a load off. It's not lazy, it's necessary. I'm sure the exhausted mom I saw carrying the backpack and scooter while pushing a stroller was already counting down the minutes until bedtime, and it wasn't even 9:00am yet. When we allow our kids to take on gradually increasing levels of responsibility, raising them becomes a little less tiring. Although it may require more upfront effort, the eventual hope is that there will be moments you can literally kick back and put your feet up as a parent, knowing that your child has this one covered.

Why All the Hovering?

Fostering independence and responsibility in children isn't always easy and will require help and reminders. Parents and teachers are the mature adults, and children will need our guidance as they grow in this area. But reminding and doing for them are two very different things. The first, reminding, is our job as the adult. The second, doing for them, is often what we do when we grow weary of that job as adults, or think our child incapable of the task. In my experience, the two main reasons parents feel the need to do everything for their children are tired resignation and over-parenting.

When we have reminded a child to hang up their backpack or put their toys away for the thousandth time, tired resignation sets in, and it can feel easier to just do it ourselves than to remind one more time. We see them throw their backpack on the ground to run off and play and just automatically assume the responsibility for picking it up ourselves. Or, we get impatient as a slow-poke child goes through their morning routine. We are tired of sounding like a broken record, so we just get everything ready for them. It is hard with a busy schedule and lots on our plate as parents to be inconvenienced by allowing the extra time for kids to do things independently. However, often what we forget during those times, is that if we will just follow through and stay patient and consistent, our child will eventually start to internalize the message that certain things are their responsibility, and we won't be inconvenienced as often.

Another reason we don't allow children to do things for themselves is thinking them incapable or worrying about them having too much responsibility. Enter the helicopter parent. This kind of parent does most things for their child because they don't think they are able or should have to. They want to shield their darlings from difficult or stressful situations at all costs, so they are ever present, hovering at the ready to do everything for their child and frankly over-parenting. Usually the helicopter parent means well and just wants to protect their children and allow them to fully enjoy childhood. To them, kids seem so little and helpless, and the parent feels there will be plenty of time for the adult world and responsibility later on.

But, the problem is, how will your children arrive at that adult world prepared without you showing them how to do things and expecting them to gradually do those things for themselves? Childhood is the time to learn independence with the safety net of parents and teachers to remind, correct, and encourage. The real world of adulthood will not be nearly so kind an educator.

Karen Spangenberg Postal, former president of the Massachusetts Psychological Association, explains the difference between helicopter parenting and lending children our more mature mental processes. She points out it is perfectly acceptable to lend children our more mature ways of doing things until they develop their own through modeling independence and responsibility. In her article on how structure improves your child's brain for Psychology Today Postal writes,

> "The helicopter parent stands at the door before school and hands their child their library book. The child never learns that they are responsible for remembering the book. A parent who lends their child a helpful structure might post a calendar near the door, where they have had their child circle each Wednesday and write "Library day" in red. This parent cues the child each morning to look at the calendar. On Wednesdays, the child sees its library day, and puts their book in their backpack. The message to the child is twofold. First, it's your responsibility to remember your book for library day, and second, here is a great way to consistently remember."[1]

Working toward Independence

As with many things in child rearing, setting clear expectations and routines from the beginning makes an enormous difference. Let's continue to use the backpack as an example. From the time a child picks out that first Tinkerbell or Iron Man backpack while school supply shopping with you, it should be made clear it is their responsibility. One way to do that is to indeed let them choose their own backpack, within limits that you determine. You could choose two or three acceptable, functional backpacks, and then give them their choice from those. It's a great way to give kids some pride in their backpack from the start. If they feel from the beginning that the backpack is completely their own, they are more likely to take responsibility for it.

Besides establishing ownership, kids will need help in defining what taking responsibility for their backpack actually looks like. Make it clear. This means they make sure to leave the house with it in the morning, they carry it to and from school, they take things out that need to be taken out, and put things in that need to be put in, and they put it away after school. I think you will be surprised at just how simple this becomes, if you consistently hold to these expectations from the start in a matter-of-fact way.

Now, if a bad habit of "Mom does everything for me" has already been established, use the beginning of the new school year or even the next week to establish a fresh start. It may take a little more time and a few reminders, but if you stay consistent and calmly stick to a new normal, eventually they will get it.

Of course, whether they are brand new to the backpack thing or need to break old habits, you are going to have to help them establish some routines in order to create true backpack independence. As stated earlier, your child may need to borrow your mental structure for order in this particular case. That means you'll need to get a structure yourself if you don't already have one. The first thing you'll need to think about is a place for your child's backpack to live. A usual resting place prevents the mad dash every morning, running from room to room to find the backpack, only to realize it was never taken out of the backseat of the car.

Next, develop some routines. Do what works for your family. If you are not at all morning people, make sure the backpack is packed and ready the night before. Lunches should be made, homework should be checked, and permission slips should be signed. This prevents the last minute rush or any early morning surprises like a note from Jessica's teacher reminding you that she needs a piece of (not yet purchased) poster board for her project tomorrow. If you're like me, the less thinking you have to do before noon, the better.

Maybe you have a busy evening schedule of sports and other extracurricular activities, and are the type of parent whose brain shuts down at 7:00pm. In that case, it may be better to set that alarm for a few minutes earlier and use that extra time in the morning to get things ready. The method doesn't matter, but consistently following it does. You will be amazed at how smoothly things go, and everyone's Monday morning will be off to a better start without screams of "Mom, where's my backpack?!?" and "Why didn't you sign my homework folder?!?"

Now, your child will inevitably have memory lapses or just plain bad judgment on the way to independence. There may be whining and carrying on at first when they are reminded to put their backpack away. They will argue with you that their room is already clean enough, or that it's not fair that they have to take out the garbage. That's ok. They don't have to understand all the reasons they are being expected to be responsible right now, or even do it happily. If you are calm, consistent, and clear, they will soon end the tantrums, realizing they aren't getting them anywhere.

Finally, to break the cycle of dependence on Mom or Dad and encourage independence and responsibility, the law of natural consequences will probably need to come into play at some point. Natural consequences are a parent's best friend. In the case of the backpack, if you really want to make it clear that your child's backpack is her responsibility; allow her to experience the consequences that might come along with not taking that responsibility seriously. For example, if she forgot to put her homework folder or library book in her backpack, then she will need to deal with the consequences. She might need to miss a privilege at school to redo homework, or not be able to check out new library books that day.

If your son is refusing to ride the scooter that he insisted on bringing to school leaving you to carry it, maybe you need to calmly inform him that if he chooses not to ride his scooter, it will stay on the sidewalk, and then someone may take it, and he won't have a scooter. We need to get comfortable as adults with allowing children to have genuine learning experiences and resist the urge to jump in to rescue them from their own consequences.

Begin With the End in Mind

While carrying your child's backpack for them may not seem like a big deal, think about the message you are sending. There are things inside the backpack which you want them to take ownership of and responsibility for—books, communication home about what's happening at school, homework, their finished work, and art projects. Early on they need the message that those things are theirs. They should be proud of them, treat them with respect, and take care of them. If they are not even physically responsible for the whereabouts and transportation of their backpack, isn't that sending them the opposite message?

When adults take on all the responsibility in a child's life, a habit of dependence starts to form. But, ultimately, I think we would all agree we want our children to grow up to be independent adults. It's often hard to remember that big picture while we're having an argument with our five-year-old for the tenth time that week to put his shoes away, or while we're running late and waiting on our pokey seven-year-old to load up their backpack. We want things to be more convenient, or to help and nurture, but the problem is we sometimes forget the point of parenting. While it's a natural, compelling instinct to want to protect your child from any hardship, it is important to keep in mind the ultimate goal in raising children.

According to psychologist Dr. Michael Thompson, the goal of parenting is to raise secure individuals who can leave the safety of their parents for the challenges that await in adulthood. Childhood requires an endpoint, and it's a parent's job to help their children arrive at that place. In fact, there are things which, no matter how badly we want to, we simply can't do for our children. In his book, Homesick and Happy: How Time Away from Parents Can Help a Child Grow, Thompson writes about eight things that parents cannot do for or give their children,

" 1. We cannot make our children happy.

2. We cannot give our children high self-esteem.

3. We cannot make friends for our children or micromanage their friendships.

4. We cannot successfully double as our child's agent, manager, and coach.

5. We cannot create the 'second family' for which our child yearns in order to facilitate his or her own growth.

6. It is increasingly apparent that we parents cannot compete with or limit our children's total immersion in the online, digital, and social media realms.

7. We cannot keep our children perfectly safe, but we can

drive them crazy trying.

8. We cannot make our children independent. (Thompson 2012. 10,11)"[2]

It is no easy task to put aside your own feelings of wanting to be needed as a parent, in order to foster the kind of independence that will be so crucial to your child's development and future success. I think if we're being honest, it's often our own emotional needs as adults we are tending to, just as much as those of our children. We understandably want them to stay little and need our help, and allowing them to do things for themselves means continually, sometimes painfully, letting go a little bit at a time.

As an outside observer of this process, I can tell you that in the classroom, kids whose parents are obviously encouraging independence at home tend to be happier, more successful students at school. Taking care of their belongings, being responsible for their work, and following through on a deadline are not foreign concepts to them. These students are carrying over the lessons learned at home in keeping their desks orderly, remembering their homework, and turning things in on time. They generally feel successful and competent, and their learning and progress reflect that.

Likewise, it is also obvious when a student is not usually expected to do things for themselves. They may not be trusted with any responsibility at home or expected to tend to their own needs, so they don't. And it is an uphill battle as a teacher to get those students to buy into the idea that responsibility and independence will be required. If they have a helicopter parent who jumps to the rescue every time they are faced with a difficult situation, they haven't developed much persistence or ability to work through a frustrating problem. They've sometimes become accustomed to pretending they can't do things so someone will do it for them. These students often need constant supervision to complete a task. Others that have never been expected to entertain themselves or do something on their own have a very difficult time working without disturbing others.

Overall the real concern is, if children do not learn independence and responsibility now, when will they? Life can be difficult and uncomfortable, and if children do not learn at an early age to tolerate and work through mild or moderate amounts of difficulty, how will they fare when faced with the real tough stuff of adulthood?

As a general rule, when you find yourself in the middle of doing something for your child, think of their future self. When you are cutting your eight-year-old's chicken into bite-sized pieces, ask yourself, "If they don't learn to do this independently now, then when?" If you are still constantly cleaning up after your twelve-year-old, ask yourself, "If they don't learn some responsibility for their things now, then when?" Finally, if you are in the habit of automatically picking up your child's backpack and carrying it for them, I beg of you to just put the backpack down.

"I couldn't possibly tell you the amount of shoes I tie in one day. Here's where the parent comes in: if you want to buy your child shoes with laces, please show/teach them how to tie them. It might take some time. Maybe practice wearing the shoes on the weekends or after school. Practice for five minutes a night, make it part of the routine. I know five-year-olds are very capable of tying their own shoes, it just takes some practice."

Jenny Harmon, Kindergarten Teacher

"Behavior and habits children learn at a young age will set the stage for characteristics such as work ethic, organization, cooperation, leadership, responsibility, and independence. These are all traits valued by those in the future who might select your child to be part of a team or organization, give them a scholarship, hire them, or fire them."

Erik Kamrath, P.E./Varsity Basketball Coach

CHAPTER THREE: *BIG EYES, BEHAVIOR, AND HOW TO KEEP YOUR COOL WHEN YOUR KIDS LOSE THEIRS*

I sat in my teacher chair at the edge of the carpet ready to give my demonstration. It was the first day of school, and I had gone over rules and expectations with my students. It was now time to discuss consequences for not following those rules and expectations.

I began by asking my kindergarteners, "Are there times a grown-up tells a kid to do something?" 21 little heads nodded yes. I asked a second question, "Are there times when that kid doesn't do what the grown-up tells them to do?" Eyes got bigger, and heads nodded yes even faster. "Well," I continued, "In our class, I know there will be times when I tell a student to do something and they might not do it. There might be times when a student is not making a good choice or forgets about an expectation, so they might just need a reminder. We all need reminders once in a while, but it doesn't mean we're in trouble. It just means we have to stop what we're doing and fix something."

"So," I explained, "If I notice you are not following an expectation, I might give you a reminder to stop and fix it without even using any words. I want to show you what my face will look like while I'm reminding you. I will not frown at you or yell, but I'll raise my eyebrows like this," I raised my eyebrows and the kids automatically mirrored my expression. "My eyes will be big, and I will not be smiling. If you see my big eyes, with my eyebrows up, and no smile, that's a clue that I mean business, and you need to stop it or fix it. It's just a chance for you to do the right thing."

Omar's hand shot up. He was sitting in the back row furthest away, still reflecting my warning face back to me exactly. His eyebrows were up, and there was not even a trace of his trademark dimples. "Yes Omar?" I called on him. In his husky little voice he said, "My mom got stop it eyes just like dat!"

All great parents and teachers have a look which communicates some variation of "knock it off" with urgency. The more calm and in control the parent or teacher is at the time, the more effective the look seems to be. Scowling or yelling at children rarely gets the desired result, and in fact just tends to ratchet up the craziness already taking place. If you don't have a look, or if yours involves a lot of wrinkle inducing facial contortions, might I recommend giving the "stop it eyes" a whirl? Next time your little pride and joy is making you less than proud, make eye contact, don't smile, and raise your eyebrows pointedly in their direction.

They will most likely look at you the same way, and then shake their head yes slowly. It tends to be a fairly easily understood, universal signal for, "You better slow your roll, and rethink that."

Bonus tip: It works on adults too. Try it with a rude fellow customer in line at the supermarket, or even your spouse. You will be amazed at how effective it is at getting your point across while remaining respectful and under control the whole time.

The Three Things I Know About Behavior

I learned about the magic in that big eyed look from my guru. She doesn't know she's my guru necessarily, but my first year teaching she was someone who finally put into words everything I believed about children, behavior, and learning. Her name is Diana Day, a fitting name for this perky, blonde Texan with big hair and an even bigger personality. She came to us as a feisty consultant, initially hired for a district workshop for new teachers on classroom management and discipline.

Her program, based on over 21 years of experience in education, was titled Vision Management, because it was about so much more than just discipline or rewards. It was a common sense approach to teaching students how to take responsibility for their actions, and basically be decent human beings. Diana focused on the big picture. She had learned that students who knew how to go about their day with self-control and positive attitudes and behaviors were obviously more successful academically and socially. She stressed talking to kids in a firm but calm and loving way, and using high expectations and order to create motivation in an optimal learning environment.

As she spoke, I couldn't help thinking how much her ideas applied to raising kids in general, and how I hoped to use her ideas with my own children one day. With the core principles I learned from Diana, and my own experience teaching 20-30 children at a time (a few of whom were bound to misbehave on any given day), I have come to three basic conclusions about children's behavior:

1. It starts with the grown-ups.

2. It's not always easy, but it's not that complicated.

3. It directly affects their academic success.

We tend to overcomplicate the reasons for misbehavior in children and what our response should be as adults. Sometimes it's just a plain old, no good, horrible, very bad day. Aliens from the Planet All Hell Breaking Loose have invaded your normally sweet child's brain, and no matter what you do or say, they are just . . . off. But more often than not, misbehavior can be attributed to something specific, and often avoided or at least headed off with a thoughtful reaction from you as a parent or teacher—if you remain clear, calm, and consistent.

Clear Expectations

When you understand some of the reasons for children's misbehavior, you can better prevent it by avoiding some causes.

One frequent cause is just a lack of direction. Maybe expectations about what is acceptable have not been laid out for that child. It is our job as the adults to teach children how to behave, and when we have not made ourselves clear about what we expect, we are often disappointed with the resulting behaviors.

Making sure you are clear and specific in your expectations, both in the classroom and at home, makes all the difference in the world. The way I viewed my role as an adult was dramatically affected when Diana Day said this,

"If you want a child to do something, you need to actually teach them how to do it."

It was brilliant, and I had never really thought of it that way before in terms of behavior. Seems like common sense to teach kids what you expect them to be able to do, but instead we often make many assumptions about what kids should be able to do. Sometimes we get frustrated as adults when children are not doing the "reasonable" thing.

For example, we think it is implied that scissors are used for cutting paper, not the hair of one's sleeping sister. We figure it goes without saying to respond with a "thank you" when somebody hands you something or a "sorry" when you walk on someone's toes. But, what I've come to learn about children is, nothing goes without saying. You need to clearly and explicitly teach a child to do anything you expect them to do on their own. Everything must be taught, modeled, and practiced before it becomes automatic.

The days I've found myself the most frustrated when working

with children are when I've been neglectful in explaining exactly what I expect. I may have introduced new materials or a new procedure for our classroom, and instead of being clear about what I expect, and giving the kids chances to practice doing it correctly, I rush ahead without making sure I've made myself clear. Then I find myself resorting to asking kids things like, "What are you doing? Why would you do that? What are you thinking?"

Even as teachers, we assume kids come to us with certain behaviors—school kinds of behaviors, like walking in a straight line, keeping their hands to themselves, or using the bathroom without turning it into a water park. But the fact of the matter is, all of these things have to be taught with the understanding that kids may have not learned them yet, or had negative behaviors unintentionally reinforced. In reality we spend a lot of time at school teaching kids how to walk in the hallway and use the bathroom appropriately. We then practice those behaviors, sometimes repeating the expectations and trying again. At home it is no different. Teach them what you want them to know, and have them practice doing it correctly.

So how do we do this? Adults need to simply and specifically explain to children what the expectations are, what following them does and does not look like, and give them ample opportunities to practice doing it correctly. An expectation is just that—expecting a certain behavior from someone on a regular basis. It's not just a list of do's and don'ts. More than that, an expectation is the normal way you want to see something done. It lays the groundwork for the general way in which we are going to proceed. Calling it an expectation implies it's something which will be automatic at a certain point, and that you are counting on the behavior to take place or not take place.

This is why my classroom rules were called expectations. Since I was the one expecting the behavior, I needed to teach them what I expected. So my students didn't come up with the expectations, but did participate in the demonstration of what those rules would look like in practice or the reasons why those rules were important. My expectations for every grade level I taught were as follows:

Keep your hands, feet, books, and other objects to yourself. At school it is very important with so many bodies, for the default to be not touching. Every item or body part one could possibly touch another person with is covered in this rule. This covers fighting, poking, pushing, shoving, but also even the "good" touching, like playing with a classmate's hair or friendly rough-housing, which is just not really appropriate for school. It draws a clear boundary for kids. It's important to cover all your bases when teaching kids specifically how to behave.

Follow directions the first time. This one is my favorite, because it is a catch-all for everything else. Basically it says that every direction I give a student needs to be followed, and it's specific in clarifying that it needs to happen without being asked more than once. If you have to be asked multiple times, or throw a tantrum on the way, you're not really following the direction.

No unkind words or gestures. Period. If it's unkind or someone might think it's unkind, don't do it. Isn't that a great rule for life in general?

Be ready to learn with all needed materials. All-encompassing because that means books, homework, writing utensils, backpack, pants, you know…the essentials

Stay with your class. Both mentally and physically you need to be with us both for your safety and learning.

The reasons these expectations work is because they are clear, specific, and all-encompassing. They speak to the greater purpose of creating a safe, loving, orderly learning environment, which I think we would agree is for the best both at home and at school. What I would do as a parent is to spend some time thinking about a few very broad, all-encompassing rules which speak to the core of what you want your home to be about. Some of them could apply to both home and school. "Follow directions the first time" is a general rule that is truly a catch all. "Stay with your class" could be modified to "Stay with your family."

Just because you have expectations doesn't mean children will not make mistakes. But if you do not have them, or do not make them clear, how can they ever meet them? Teaching a child to do something doesn't guarantee they will do it perfectly every time. Teaching anything requires re-teaching and practice. We wouldn't teach a child multiplication or division and expect them to get it right away, or do it perfectly every time.

Behavior is the same way. Any child is bound to misbehave, but often that inevitability is used as an excuse for adults not having high expectations for them. Just because they won't be able to do it perfectly right away or every time, does not mean it is not important for them to know and worthy of being taught. I think many parents and teachers use the fact that a child is young, or tired, or frustrated, as an excuse for their behavior instead of using it as an opportunity to teach them a better way. Kids are looking to adults for structure and limits. They want us to be the boss and help make their world a less confusing place by framing life lessons clearly for them, since we're the ones with the experience.

Keep Calm & Carry On

Have you ever noticed how chaos tends to be contagious? Often a child's misbehavior causes or is a result of chaos around them. A kid is freaking out, which causes the adult to freak out, which in turn causes the kid to freak out more, and we're in a vicious cycle. Kids don't automatically know how to regulate their own emotions. They need to be taught, and so they're counting on us as adults to be calm and keep it together.

What do we think when we see somebody completely losing it? We think they may be overreacting, immature, or have possibly forgotten to take their meds that morning. However, nobody would look at them and think, "Wow. You are really in control of that situation." Yelling, screaming, and otherwise carrying on are not the trademarks of someone who is in control. In fact they communicate the opposite. The person has lost their cool, along with any control of the situation, which is clearly beyond him or her. Kids notice it too. When adults are yelling, angry, and emotional, it is clear to them the adults are not in control of that situation. Keeping calm is key.

Now, stuff happens. We lose our cool as adults from time to time, and I am not suggesting you aren't going to have an emotion about the fact that your child just colored all over their walls with permanent marker, or said, "Mommy" for the 4,532nd time since lunch. But to be effective in discipline, the biggest thing I have learned in the classroom is that calm wins every time. In fact, it takes children by surprise and grabs their attention when they are behaving erratically, but you are completely calm, cool, and collected.

When it comes to behavior, we tend to operate in extremes thinking the only two options are to be mean and aggressive or sweet and coddling. That is simply not the case. In my experience, it is absolutely possible, and most effective, to be calm, but assertive to encourage the behavior you want to see in children. Here are eight things I do in the classroom, and you can do at home, to keep your cool when your kids are losing theirs:

Make eye contact. Lean in so you are at their level, to let them know you mean business while talking.

Keep your volume low. If you are loud, they will get loud, and the whole situation will escalate according to the volume.

Speak slowly. Put space between your words for emphasis instead of yelling. For example, "You. . . are. . . bothering. . . the. . . cat. . . when. . . you. . . carry. . . her. . . around. . . Put. . . her. . . down. . . now. . . please. . . before. . . she. . . bites. . . your. . . lips. . . off."

Fake it if you have to. You may be seething inside, but take a deep breath, and remember you are the grown-up. Act like the adult you want them to become.

Agree to disagree. Kids don't have to like what we're telling them to do. We often are upset when children don't see things our way. They don't always need to, and may not yet be capable of understanding. They are still learning, and probably won't see the value in a particular behavior until later on in life. We need to be ok with our kids being upset with us once in a while. A child doesn't have to agree with you to do what they're told. Stop trying to convince and matter-of-factly, without loaded questions and guilt tripping, tell them what you need them to do.

Don't engage in the craziness. It is so hard not to enter into a power struggle sometimes. Waiting until your child is calm, and using as few words as possible, authoritatively state what they did wrong, what they should have done, and welcome them back to the land of sanity.

Walk away. Ignoring behavior which is clearly attention-seeking is something the only way. But walking way also prevents a power struggle if you can calmly state what they need to do and then get out of their way. Often if left alone, and if they see you are unwilling to engage in an argument with them, kids will end up fixing their behavior. Nagging, lecturing, or arguing with them doesn't work.

Remember, their feelings don't have to be yours. Their tantrum or misbehavior is a choice they made, and it's your job to teach them a better way. That's simply all it is. Don't let it ruin your day.

Consistency is Key

Finally, one of the biggest reasons I see for misbehaving kids is inconsistent adults. A little boy named Alex reminded me of how much consistency matters a few years back. When I was teaching kindergarten, I had places where students could go to refocus. These refocus areas were another trick I learned from Diana Day and were used after the Stop It Eyes had already been employed numerous times. They were not time-outs, but alternate locations to learn from where students knew they were expected to think about how to fix their behavior. As such, I had them in various locations throughout the classroom. If we were working at the tables and a student needed to be away from others to concentrate, they moved to The Thinking Table to do their work. If the class was at the carpet, and a student needed some more space to focus, they sat on one of the tile squares just off the carpet, a Thinking Square. If they needed a chair, they went to the Thinking Chair.

It was made clear from the beginning of the school year that it was not a punishment. The students helped to name the locations, and in fact could move to one of those locations themselves if they just needed to be alone or have some space, and come back to the group when they were ready.

But, if I saw they needed to think about how to fix a certain behavior, and I asked them to go to one of those spots, they understood we would have to have a conversation about what expectation they were not following, and what they should have done differently, before they were welcomed back to the group for another chance. There was no magic time limit, because it was not a traditional time-out. Students knew to just prepare themselves there, and I would be there for a private conversation when I got a chance. If they were upset, refusing to talk, or disrespectful when I went to them, I would simply walk away saying, "I see you need more time."

One particular afternoon, I sent Alex to the Thinking Chair for not keeping his hands to himself at the carpet. He went, and as usual, I went about my teaching to finish up the lesson before stopping to have a conversation with him. About a minute later, however, I glanced at the clock and realized we were late for our library time. So, I told the kids to quickly line up at the door with their library books. I shut off the lights, and we filed out the door.

As we got to the library, panic grabbed me as I realized Alex was not with us. I left the students with the librarian and rushed back to the classroom, where I found Alex obediently sitting in his chair. Frustrated, I started to lecture him on the importance of staying with the class and paying attention. "But Mrs. Ladd," he interrupted. "We didn't have a talk about my behavior, so I was still thinking."

While I was frustrated with Alex for taking things quite so literally, I was also reminded about how much consistency matters. The students in my class knew if they were sent to a refocus area, we would be having a conversation about it every single time, and that it needed to happen before they rejoined the group. So in fairness, it was my fault for being too rushed to follow through on what I had told them was going to happen, and what they had grown accustomed to.

I have an unfortunate secret to tell you. There is no magic formula to get kids to behave. No complicated system of sticker charts, rewards, and consequences is going to ensure perfect behavior. Even if some ideas work better than others, the key to any strategy being effective is consistency. This is not always fun. It requires self-control and following through when you don't feel like it. It takes many repetitions of a correct behavior before it becomes the norm, but it only takes one time of not following through on what you said for kids to believe you don't mean what you say. So as a teacher or a parent, our focus should be on using whatever behavior philosophy we believe in clearly, calmly, and consistently.

We Need Each Other

On top of consistency in how each of us manages behavior in our own individual spheres of home and school, consistency between home and school is also vital to student success. Effective behavioral education is about more than just avoiding "bad" behavior and rewarding "good" behavior. It is about kids developing self-awareness and self-management, social awareness and skills, and eventually becoming adults that maintain healthy relationships and make responsible choices. Since a child spends so much time in both places, instilling these values cannot be accomplished at home or school alone.

You might have been reading these ideas about behavior management thinking, "Why does how I parent my child matter to her or any other teacher?" or, "Isn't it my business how I deal with disciplining my own child?" Absolutely, it is. As I've said before, you are your child's first and most important teacher. But, that's exactly why I care—because in all seriousness you have tremendous influence over your child's behavior, and their success in my classroom depends on it. The biggest challenges I have faced in the classroom have nothing to do with kids' ability to learn and everything to do with kids' ability to behave. A child who has learned self-control, patience, and social skills has so many more tools in their arsenal when they face an academic challenge than a child who is already struggling just to behave appropriately. Nobody learns well in a disruptive environment, and respect is essential for teachers to teach and students to learn. Kids learn to respect their teachers and other adults at school by first learning to respect their parents at home.

I also care because I see so many parents doing it the hard way. They're stressed and exhausted by their kid's behavior and as someone who spends eight hours a day with those same kids, I want to offer some help and insight. So, the bottom line of this chapter is to ask for your help and hopefully give you some assistance in return. The way I see it, I need you and you need me. We are both influential adults in the life of children. We're on the same team—this team of adults teaching your child about the world and how to exist in it—so we are in this thing together. It's not 'me vs. you,' but sometimes it's 'us vs. them'— them being those little people who have the ability to hold big people hostage with tantrums and bring us to our knees with meltdowns. We need to band together.

My first job as a teacher is to create and maintain a safe, nurturing, respectful environment purposely designed for learning, and I know you would agree with that priority. As communities we spend millions on the latest research-based materials for our kids. We shop for schools based on their athletic opportunities and technological offerings. I would argue we need to invest just as much in creating environments together where students are respected and learn to respect, where they are cared for and learn to care for others, where they learn patience, self-control, and kindness as crucial traits for accomplishing great things. It starts with us as the adults. It's not that complicated, and our kids' futures depend on it.

> "Acceptable behavior is learned early in a child's life, and he or she will carry this behavior into their adult years. Make sure the behavior you want to see in your twenty-five year old is being taught to your five year old."
>
> ***Vicki Sharkey, First Grade Teacher***

CHAPTER FOUR: *RECESS, SOCIAL SKILLS, AND THE TRUTH ABOUT BULLYING*

Htay's family was brand new to the country from a refugee camp in Burma. They had been sponsored by a local church to come to the United States, and had just arrived. The school secretary told me a little bit about the family after she had registered them earlier in the week, placing Htay in my kindergarten Sheltered English Immersion class. I didn't really expect to see them on Meet the Teacher Night, since they were brand new to the country, and understandably had many other things to concern themselves with. But just as I was starting to pack up for the night, Htay shyly entered my room, holding her mother's hand and so much wisdom in her small half smile.

Monica, an American woman who towered over Htay and her mother, immediately introduced herself, explaining she was kind of the liaison from the church to help Htay's family navigate this new country and make sure they had what they needed. Htay and her mother knew not a word of English, and so I mostly spoke to Monica, and together we used lots of hand motions and visuals to try to convey the necessary information.

Meanwhile, Htay wandered over to the classroom library area and contentedly sat down on one of the small red chairs. She paged through books while Monica told me she would be making sure to get all the necessary supplies and help fill out forms. When it was time to leave, Htay did not want to go, pointing excitedly at all the illustrations on every book cover, seemingly unable to believe her eyes at all the beautiful pictures.

Htay quietly and bravely started school the next day with the rest of my class. Monica stopped in a few times a week at their house to help read notes from school and make sure she had what she needed. My class was comprised entirely of English language learners, who spoke a variety of languages other than English as their first. I joked that I had a mini United Nations going on in my room. With a wide range of languages and cultures represented, we had a natural place for so many conversations and teachable moments about differences and being kind to each other. With all these opportunities to practice accepting each other and our unique qualities, Htay fit in just fine, and gradually began to make friends. Sometimes no words are needed, and friendship at that age can be built on a mutual passion for play dough and playground sand.

October rolled around, and it was time for the perennial kindergarten field trip to the pumpkin farm. The kids were supposed to bring a bag lunch from home, and since Htay usually ate school lunch, I made sure to call Monica earlier in the week to let her know Htay's mom needed to send her with a lunch that day. At the farm, after corn mazes and hayrides, all the kindergarten classes settled in at picnic tables, unpacking sandwiches, Cheetos, and Capri Suns. I had packed a few extra things, in case something was lost in translation or anyone had forgotten a lunch, but everyone including Htay seemed to have a lunch. Just as I was biting into my own peanut butter and jelly sandwich, I noticed Htay out of the corner of my eye. She had brought rice and an entire smoked fish, eyeballs and all, both of which she was happily picking away at with her fingers.

A few of the kids noticed too, and I immediately began to get a little panicky. I internally prepared my best quick talk about accepting differences, and was ready to jump to Htay's defense if any of my students started to make fun of her unusual lunch. To, my pleasant surprise no one did! I saw Manuel, sitting to her right, look at Htay with her fish and rice. He simply shrugged his shoulders, and then bit into his own sandwich, stuffed with peppers and avocado, without so much as a giggle. That scene at a picnic table on an October afternoon sticks with me to this day as an example of how accepting children truly are, and how fascinating and inspiring their social interactions can be.

Welcome to the Jungle Gym

As a teacher, some of the most frequent questions I get from parents center around those social interactions and of course, recess. Moms and Dads want to know, "Is she playing with anyone at recess? Is he the kid sitting all alone? Why does he keep getting hurt at recess? Is she being bossy, rough, or excluding others on the playground? Who's supervising at recess? Is he playing fair?" School is not just about reading, math, and learning to write. Even as adults, some of the childhood moments which are most clearly burned into our memories revolve around recess, and it's natural for parents to be concerned and interested in their child's safety and social development. However, I don't want you to have to be the creepy mom who slowly drives by the playground conveniently at recess time to watch over your darling, so I will give you a little peek at the happenings on the playground from the teacher's point of view.

First of all, just realize there will be many children outside at the same time. This can be a little overwhelming for kids when first starting school, and it may take them a few weeks before they're comfortable joining in a game or making new friends. Or, they may be the type to chat for the entire time with two or three friends while calmly strolling the playground. Some kids just like to bring a book out and read in the shade. All of these things are ok and normal, as the main purpose of recess should be to provide an unstructured break time.

Usually students from multiple classrooms, and possibly even different grade levels share the playground during recess. It's a great chance for your child to interact with other kids who are different from them. Unlike a play date, it may be one of their first opportunities to learn how to get along with others who they may not have otherwise played with or chosen to work with.

Because there are so many children, there might be rules for recess which wouldn't be necessary at home with siblings, or just a few neighborhood kids at the park. For example, one year I had to make a "no tag or chasing each other" rule. While there is absolutely nothing inherently wrong with tag or chase, that class of kids just couldn't handle it. It was a particularly grabby, physical group, and things quickly deteriorated into tackle tag. After many chances we just had an honest talk one day about how I was noticing most of the incidents of getting in trouble or hurt at recess involved tag or chasing, and so we were going to agree not to do those things at recess for a time while we fixed that problem. After much work on keeping our hands and feet to ourselves, and being gentle with friends, we were able to reinstitute tag.

Even with precautions and rules for safety, kids will occasionally get hurt. Adults are present for emergencies and to help kids make safe choices, but nobody can foresee and prevent all injuries when kids are playing. With many children on the playground at the same time, it is impossible to monitor any one child constantly. If that kind of supervision seems to be necessary for your child, there needs to be an honest conversation among parents, teachers, and administration about a strategy to ensure your child is safe and successful socially beyond just, "the teacher needs to watch my kid at every moment." It is setting both the child and the teacher up for failure, because that is an impossible task.

Given the necessary break from learning and structured time recess provides, taking away recess should not be used as a punishment in my opinion. Teachers don't always agree on this, and my own opinion has definitely changed over time. However, unless it is an issue of the safety of a child or others, and there is a specific plan in place to teach appropriate behavior and allow for another try, taking away recess should not be an option.

Students may need a mandated break for a minute to settle down after an altercation, and should absolutely be stopped to have conversations with teachers about fixing inappropriate behavior. However, more often than not, the kids who get recess taken away for misbehavior or unfinished work throughout the day are those who need it the most, so it becomes a vicious cycle. I think if a teacher is constantly finding themselves keeping a child in to do incomplete work, or if that child has lost recess repeatedly for behaviors unrelated to recess, it's pretty clear that it's not an effective strategy. The teacher needs to take a closer look at the problem. Merely punishing a child for a certain behavior does not necessarily change that behavior.

Besides individually taking away recess, many schools and districts are drastically limiting the amount of free play time students get, citing the need for increased time spent on teaching academics. If your child's school is getting rid of recess, it's worth the battle to fight it as a parent. While I understand the pressure on schools to squeeze every instructional minute out of the day, it is counterproductive to eliminate recess. Nobody is productive without a break. It is completely inappropriate to have children (or anyone for that matter) cooped up indoors for eight hours a day without a chance for an unstructured brain break. Play is where learning happens in childhood, and we should encourage the chance for kids to run off some energy while using imagination and learning important social skills.

Why I Don't Believe in Bullying

When discussing kids' social interactions and recess, bullying is one of the first concerns brought up. Bullying has become a loaded word in our society. The media warns parents to worry about their child being bullied and teachers to respond strongly to bullying. It's politically correct and even popular to express shock and outrage about acts of cruelty taking place in our schools, and then to propose a mandated solution. We need to look like we're doing something about it. Schools have adopted zero tolerance policies in relation to bullying. School districts are purchasing entire anti-bullying programs with expensive curriculum and training. Parents and teachers have developed a heightened sensitivity to any negative interaction which could be construed as bullying. Labels like bully, bystander, and victim are doled out, and children are cast to play out these roles in a playground drama.

Some of it is understandable. As parents we want to keep our children safe, and raise them to be kind to one another. Parents want to know what to do if their child is being bullied or (gasp) is the bully. Teachers fear the phone call from a parent, informing us that their child is being bullied and accusing us of doing nothing about it.

But often as adults we are also unwilling to have the real conversations necessary. We want to solve the mystery of children being mean to one another while ignoring adults doing the very same thing. We think if we use the right buzz words, and have a specific program and more education around the topic, bullying can be prevented. While many of these things are well-intentioned, we're asking many of the wrong questions when it comes to bullying, and answering them with incomplete solutions. As one of my favorite authors, Glennon Doyle Melton points out in her book, Carry On, Warrior: Thoughts on Life Unarmed,

> "The acceptable response seems to be that we should better educate students and teachers about what bullying is and how to react to it appropriately. This plan is positive, certainly. But on its own, it seems a little like bailing frantically without first looking for the hole in the boat"(Melton 2013, 137).[1]

Where Did Kids Learn That?

"Kids are cruel." "School is brutal." "Watch out for those mean girls." Any of these sentiments are commonplace in our discussion around the social life of kids. I have to tell you, in my experience, children are not exceptionally cruel. In fact if you've ever spent any length of time with them, you'll realize they seem to have a larger capacity for acceptance and unconditional love than most adults. I also do not buy into the "mean girl" mentality. I don't believe that being a girl of a certain age means you will automatically be either a mean girl, or a girl bullied by said mean girls. I do believe that developmentally, at a certain age, children are figuring out who they are in the world. Social interactions and what others think of them become extremely important, and sometimes kids need guidance to navigate those waters. I think we all have the capability to be mean, to leave others out, to gossip. Adolescent girls, or kids on the playground do not have the monopoly on mean. Melton continues,

> "Each time these stories are reported, the sound bite is: 'kids can be so cruel.' This is something we tend to say: kids these days, they can be so cruel. But I think this is just a phrase we toss around to excuse ourselves from facing the truth. I don't think kids are any crueler than adults. I just think kids are less adept at disguising their cruelty"(Melton, 2013, 137).[1]

Whether we do it consciously or by example, adults teach children how to treat each other. They overhear our phone conversations or the way we gossip about other adults during a play date. They watch our reactions to the evening news about people who are "different" or "other." They might even be in earshot of teachers badmouthing other staff members and parents on the playground during recess, and while they may not understand every detail, they notice disrespect, segregation, and aggression in the media.

Undoubtedly, children unfortunately witness adults behaving in all kinds of nasty ways toward one another, and while we might try to disguise it with humor, religion, or complicated politics, our actions speak louder than words.

> "Children are not cruel. Children are mirrors. They want to be 'grownup,' so they act how grown-ups act when we think they're not looking. They do not act how we tell them to act at school assemblies. They act how we really act. They believe what we believe. They say what we say. . . The only difference is that children bully in the hallways and the cafeterias while we bully from behind pulpits and legislative benches and sitcom one-liners"(Melton, 2013, 137-38).[1]

The most important role we can play as adults then, instead of vigilantly searching for bullies or bullying behavior, should be to watch the example we are setting to teach children how to treat each other with kindness and respect. If we do that, we've got the bullying problem covered.

Beyond setting an example, I think our second most important role as adults in preventing bullying is in how we respond to inappropriate behavior from kids. I think if we calmly, consistently taught children how to treat one another and calmly, consistently applied appropriate consequences when they were not treating each other kindly, bullying wouldn't really be an issue.

If you really think about it, part of the aggression of bullying lies in the repetition of an offense. Usually one time acts are not considered bullying. I think one reason certain situations turn into bullying scenarios is that at the very beginning, when an inappropriate behavior was first noticed, nothing was done about it.

For example, when one student was bothering another, the teacher may have been too busy to deal with it. Maybe it was easier to turn the other way on the playground than pull that child aside to have a conversation. Another child's aggressive behavior in their own house might have been chalked up to "boys being boys" instead of discussing how some people don't like it when you jump on their head. Kids are allowed to be pushy and grabby with each other because, "Well they're little and don't know better," but then they become bigger and we call it bullying, not having done much in the meantime to teach them a better way.

I asked parents about their thoughts on kids' social interactions and bullying. Becky, a friend of mine with preschool-aged kids, responded with a great point about her daughter, Liberty.

"One thing that we've always taught Liberty, but that

ERICA LADD

doesn't seem to be talked about very often, is not to bug or bother people. We had to address this in preschool when the whole "keep your hands to yourself" rule was introduced during group mat time. She never was harmful but would explore other kids outfits (oh the sparkles), or bump elbows because they were squished."

Especially at a young age, Liberty's actions are completely normal, but Becky and her husband know the importance of showing their child how to interact socially. They are proactive to teach Liberty a better way.

The Problem with Bully Talk

Have you noticed we've become a smidge bullying obsessed as a society? We have created an entire culture around the concept of bullying and rallying against it. Everyone is on the anti-bully bandwagon, from cartoon characters to Real Housewives of Orange County. Is there a specific colored anti-bullying ribbon for celebrities to wear at award shows yet?

What defines bullying, anyway? I would argue bullying seems to be getting worse because we've expanded the definition to include any time a kid does anything unkind to another kid. Normal childhood arguments and problems are now labeled as bullying, and we've decided we need a program to fix it, which involves calling out bullies and defending victims. No wonder we're a bit panicked about it when everywhere you turn you hear or read

66

the word bully; often linked to depression and even suicide in victims.

Sometimes it's easier to focus on this broad, vague problem of bullying instead of addressing little problems as they arise. I think what we're really doing is turning a blind eye to many unacceptable actions from kids along the way, and then reacting when a situation has turned volatile or is recurring. Now someone has become a victim and is accusing a bully. Many would have you believe there is a dramatic increase in bullying in our schools and among our children, but as Dr. Susan Eva Porter argues in her book, Bully Nation: Why America's Approach to Childhood Aggression is Bad for Everyone,

> "The broader definition of bullying accounts for much of the supposed increase we are seeing in bullying behavior in our culture. Adults often ask me if kids today are worse than those of previous generations. My answer is an emphatic no. Kids haven't changed, but our definitions of their negative behaviors have, and this has had a profound effect on how they think about themselves and their relationships with their peers"(Porter,2013)[2]

In her book, she goes on to explain the three major problems she has noticed in her experience as a principal with the hyper-vigilance around bullying and the loaded language around the topic. Besides expanding the definition of bullying, current bully language is damaging and ineffective for the children involved, and we are expecting kids to behave in ways they are not developmentally ready for (Porter, 2013).

Something is happening, which is really quite troubling. Where certain behaviors are concerned, we are labeling kids as bullies instead of simply a child who is making a bad choice. We are condemning children because of childhood mistakes or aggressive behavior they might be struggling with, instead of helping them along in their social development.

To put it in perspective, we would all agree behaviors like stealing, hitting, and lying are unacceptable. But, we know they are fairly common in childhood, and things we need to repeatedly teach children not to do. Developmentally, with guidance and appropriate consequences, we know they often mature and understand those behaviors are wrong. We would never dream of labeling a child as a pathological liar because they lie a few times as a small child. We would not call a child who steals a piece of candy a thief, and enroll them in a special program for young kleptomaniacs. So why are we so quick to label children who struggle to interact appropriately with other children as bullies, and treat them as lifelong offenders in need of dramatic intervention?

By slapping the label of "bully" on a child and branding a particular group of behaviors "bullying," we are implying those behaviors are beyond the scope of normal. Even the Department of Health and Human Services has officially broadened their definition of bullying to include behaviors like spitting, name-calling, and leaving someone out on purpose. I am not suggesting those behaviors are not hurtful and wrong, or that we should not deal with them as such. However, to have an honest conversation about bullying, we need to put down our knee-jerk reactions for a moment to all kinds of kid misbehaviors which are not actually bullying, just kids making mistakes, and needing correction.

Bothering other children at the carpet, having a hard time keeping our hands to ourselves, or excluding another child on the playground are not necessarily bullying. They are bothering, touching, and excluding. By sticking all of those actions under the big umbrella of bullying, we make misbehavior a vague mystery to kids. Instead we should identify specific behaviors, how they affect other people, allow children to experience an appropriate consequence, and work with them on what to do differently. Just like any behavior, that does not guarantee kids will always get it right, but zero tolerance for normal childhood behaviors too quickly becomes zero tolerance for the children who display them.

My niece Emma summed it up best in her opinion on a new boy in her kindergarten class. She was telling my brother about this boy, how he didn't follow directions and wasn't very nice to the other kids in class. When my brother asked if he was a bully, Emma replied, "No daddy. He's not a bully. He's just new around here and doesn't know how we do things yet." I think if we all took this approach to kids, we might have fewer bullies and fewer victims.

Parents, I understand that the thought of what your kids will face as they grow socially can be scary. But, before you decide to send your child to a remote island to be individually homeschooled by a monk so they can avoid all of this nonsense, I want you to know it's really up to us as the adults once again. School can be a social shark tank or a place where students develop meaningful relationships and grow socially. It depends on how we frame it, and what we do to teach our little ones about what it means to be human and treat others as such.

"My views on taking recess away have evolved over the years. I don't use it to have students finish work anymore. If there are social or behavioral issues that need to be addressed, I'll have a student take a minute or two to think about the issue at hand, and then we briefly talk about it and come up with an action plan if necessary."

Heidi Evans, First Grade Teacher

"There need to be consistent guidelines and monitoring of negative behaviors, but labeling some behaviors can prevent kids from learning how to compete, be passionate, assertive, ambitious, and for athletic purposes – even aggressive!"

Amber Clark, High School Special Ed. Teacher

CHAPTER FIVE: *CONFERENCES, COMMUNICATION, AND HOW TO FIND THE SAME PAGE*

In the middle of my lesson on plural nouns one afternoon, I looked up to find the assistant principal waiting at my classroom door. With her usual walkie-talkie in one hand, she waved me over with the other to indicate she needed a minute. I gave my second graders a job to make a list of all the plural nouns they could think of on whiteboards with a partner, before I nervously headed to the door. The assistant principal, Mrs. White, was lovely. But it usually indicated a problem with a student or parent if she "needed a minute."

When I got to the door, she handed me a neon post-it note with a parent's name and phone number on it. Apparently Mrs. Dexter, the mother of my student, Carlie, had entered the office in fits just a few minutes earlier. Carlie and her family were new to the school that year; a military family who had just recently moved from across the country. Mrs. Dexter was a very sweet PTO mom who had never indicated any problems with the school or her daughter's class in the past. But that day she had been fuming mad and red in the face as she demanded to speak to an administrator immediately. Mrs. White had been surprised to see her so upset.

Mrs. Dexter was not happy about all kinds of things, from a lack of information sent home about homework and spelling lists, to not knowing when class events and parties were. She accused me of not communicating with her about Carlie's performance or telling her when there had been a change in the school schedule. She said the last straw was when she had no idea it had been an early dismissal the day before, meaning nobody was home when Carlie got there at 1:50, so she had to wait outside alone for two hours.

I was dumbfounded. I insisted to Mrs. White I had never heard one word about any of this from this parent, and was just as surprised as she was that Mrs. Dexter was so upset. I also assured her I had sent numerous emails on all the topics she had claimed to get no information about. I didn't understand what the problem was.

Mrs. White sighed and pointed at the note saying, "Well, I told her I would talk with you, and that you would be giving her a call as soon as you got a chance. Maybe there's been some sort of misunderstanding."

I nodded and agreed to call her after school. When I did, Mrs. Dexter launched into an obviously upset version of what I had already heard from Mrs. White. I explained to Mrs. Dexter that I had been sending emails to her about all of these things, but she swore she hadn't received any of them. Feeling a bit defensive at this point, I checked the email address I had on file for her and read it back to her over the phone, making sure I had the right address.

"Oh!" she sounded surprised. "That's my husband's email address, and he is deployed right now. How did you get that address?"

I had met Carlie's dad at the beginning of the school year, but knew he had very recently been deployed overseas. "It's on the student information card you filled out on Meet the Teacher Night."

There was silence on the other end.

I broke it first, "At the beginning of the year, I just entered all of the addresses into my email contacts, and have been sending emails to that one ever since. That would explain why you think I haven't been communicating with you. I understand your frustration now. Would there be a time before school one morning this week that you could come in to meet quickly? I can answer any questions you might have and clear things up for you."

In barely a whisper Mrs. Dexter replied, "Yes, I'd like that. Thank you. How about tomorrow?"

I met with her the next morning and expressed how sorry I was about the miscommunication. She also apologized for not saying something to me sooner and for the misunderstanding. I felt awful that she had spent these past three months thinking I was not telling her any important information, or worse yet that I didn't care enough about Carlie to convey how she was doing. Through that embarrassed conversation, and a few others in the years to follow, I learned a few important lessons about communication and how parents and teachers can get, and stay, on the same page.

Go to the Source

Carlie's mom was understandably upset. She had missed monthly newsletters, mass parent emails, and even detailed progress updates about her daughter's performance, all because I had the wrong email address on file. It was a problem which could have easily been cleared up had she given me a call or emailed me herself. But she never spoke a word of it to me and instead went straight to my boss. Going directly to the teacher first with any concerns is always a better choice for a few reasons.

First of all, it shows respect for the teacher to go to her first, offering her the benefit of the doubt. There could just be a simple misunderstanding, and speaking to her first would give her the chance to clear it up. Or, there could be a legitimate problem. Teachers are human and make mistakes. There is no such thing as a perfect school year. If a teacher has caused a problem, or something is bothering you or your child, the teacher wants to know about it, and be given the opportunity to correct the issue herself. It may require further involvement, but at least you have given her the courtesy of going to her first, and can then take appropriate next steps up the chain of command if you are dissatisfied with the outcome.

Second, going directly to the teacher focuses on a solution. We need to be solution-oriented instead of simply focusing on the problem or venting about something we're unhappy with. When parents complain about a teacher to other parents or to the principal, it's really about "getting the teacher in trouble," and rarely about solving the actual problem. Even if you have good reason to be upset, going that route does not tend to be helpful in getting to the root of the issue or fixing it. The goal should be making the person who is directly involved with the concern aware of it, and then working together to solve it as a team. Taking up a defensive posture of parent vs. teacher is ineffective and tends to cause even more problems.

Finally, going directly to the teacher with the concern solves the problem at hand quickly before it is blown out of proportion. Had Carlie's mom come to me right away, many months of resentment would not have built up, and we could have made sure she had the information she needed right away. Instead, she continued to miss out on valuable classroom news and felt ignored and hurt. Additionally, if a child is struggling with a concept or the way it's being taught, that information is also important to know as soon as possible. Teachers need to know when a child is having difficulty in order to support that student immediately.

We teachers also need to go directly to the source. I've learned that I need to contact a parent with any concerns I have as soon as possible. When I didn't hear back from Mrs. Dexter after sending emails, I assumed no news was good news and quickly forgot about it. If I had paid closer attention and called her directly after I had not heard from her in a while, I might have saved us all some confusion and frustration along the way.

Have an Actual Conversation

Although modern technology like email is great for quick communication and convenient sharing of information, nothing beats a good old-fashioned conversation when it comes to parent/teacher communication.

One year, I had a particularly. . . shall we say. . . involved mother. Her child required lots of support, and she was very specific about what that support should look like. I would receive page long emails multiple times a day, many of them contentious because of something she perceived to be lacking in how I was doing my job. Often these emails were copied to my principal and even the district superintendent. At first I was angry, defensive, and quite frankly terrified of her. Her demands seemed impossible, and she seemed to have very unrealistic expectations. I felt like there was no pleasing her. After one particularly scathing email from her, I decided to pick up the phone. To be honest with you, I had avoided talking to her in person, because I was scared of her. But,

I also knew she was printing out and keeping all my emails as formal documentation, and it was clear she wasn't pleased. So I decided to just give her a call instead of providing another email from me to add to the "Ammunition Against Mrs. Ladd" file. I'd had enough of the email back and forth at that point, so I thought an informal conversation might be the way to go.

I started the phone call with a simple, "I just got your email, and I know you have some concerns. I'd love to talk with you about them if you have a minute."

Right away her tone softened dramatically from that in the email. She sincerely thanked me for getting back to her so quickly, and for the first time I felt I was able to explain myself clearly, and build some trust to make progress in our relationship as partners in her son's education.

The personal phone call was powerful for a few reasons. First of all, it showed that I cared. Personal attention in the form of a phone conversation or face to face meeting shows you respect the other person and care about their concerns. Sometimes just being willing to take time out of your schedule, sit down, and talk, goes a long way in defusing a situation. Talking it out is more informal and often lightens the mood in a tense moment.

Another important benefit to a personal conversation is that a lot of misunderstanding can be avoided. It can be very hard to read someone's tone in an email or note, and even covering your message in smiling emoticons does not guarantee your innocent question will not be misinterpreted by the reader. Things can come across accusatory or irritated via email, even when it's not intentional. I have been guilty of sending off an email in a busy rush and regretting it when I later realize it sounded harsh or calloused.

I've found that when I talk with a parent on the phone or in person, we both walk away feeling like we actually understand each other better. A dad can hear in my voice that I'm not too mean or strict, but just want what's best for his child. When talking to a busy mom on the phone, I can hear the other kids screaming at home in the background and understand she has a lot on her plate. Through that conversation, I began to see how the mother I was struggling to please was not just unreasonable or unrealistic, but trying to maintain high expectations for her son, which nobody would fault her for. During a meeting, I might be able to show a mom an example of the kind of work causing her child some difficulty during a face to face meeting. Through an actual conversation, questions can be asked, and expectations can be clarified.

However, calling someone or meeting face to face isn't always an immediate option. In those cases, email can be a great tool in setting up just such a conversation. Even if I don't have time to talk at the moment, but want to make sure to acknowledge a parent's concerns quickly, I send a quick email just letting them know I would love to schedule a phone call or meeting at their earliest convenience. Remember, email is great for asking a general question or sending off a quick note, but if you are finding yourself firing off a frustrated email to your child's teacher, stop and think about it. This might be a better approach:

> Good afternoon Mrs. Ladd,
>
> I need to talk with you as soon as possible about some concerns I have about. . .
>
> When might be a good time for a phone call or meeting?
>
> Thanks for your time,
>
> Mrs. Smith
>
> 321-5467

A short email gives the teacher a heads up and some time to prepare herself to bring any relevant information to the conversation, because she knows what you would like to talk about. Since she is busy teaching all day, it also allows her to give you her full attention at a time when you can have a private conversation. A little bit of notice ensures you won't catch her off guard with only three minutes to spare before she needs to get to a staff meeting, or pick up her students from lunch.

Finally, an actual conversation is so important because it's an open dialogue, instead of a one-way street. Unlike email, it allows for problems to be openly discussed and resolved together. Often times people shy away from direct communication to avoid conflict. But, in the end, truly collaborative solutions to a problem are much more likely when we put down our defenses and step away from our keyboards.

Build a Relationship

Effective parent/teacher communication is based on a mutually respectful relationship. Relationships are not automatic. They are built over time through friendly chats and difficult conversations alike. Kindness really is the key. Let your child's teachers know how much you see and appreciate the time and effort they pour into your child. Send teachers encouraging notes or emails once in a while. If something they are doing really works well for your child, let them know. If you're seeing that your child is struggling with a subject at home, tell their teachers. Don't wait until you have a major concern or problem. Talk about what you notice, and treat teachers like the valuable partners they are in your child's overall education. Frequent, positive communication builds a trusting relationship.

That being said, it's also important to be realistic. Teachers have many students and by extension, many families to communicate with. To you, your child is the world, which is just as it should be. But keep in mind, there are quite a few kids in the teacher's world, all of which require attention and support, some more than others. This is not an excuse for an incompetent teacher to ignore you or your child, but I beg of you to be realistic in your expectations. If you send an email in the morning, realize your child's teacher is teaching all day and might not see it until lunch, after school, or the next morning. I think 24 hours is a reasonable amount of time to wait before expecting a reply to a phone message or email. Even then, if you have not heard back within 24 hours, try one more time. We all know what it's like to have a particularly chaotic day, and when you throw 30 kids into the mix, the chaos multiplies for a teacher. Give the teacher the benefit of the doubt before you storm into the principal's office claiming that she is ignoring you.

Do's and Don'ts of Talking with Teachers

Communication between home and school is so important to student success, but it can be tricky. I know I speak for many teachers in admitting that sometimes one of the most difficult, but important, parts of the job can be maintaining positive parent relationships. Parents and teachers step on each other's toes without really meaning to. The conversation often seems to get off on the wrong foot, and both the parent and teacher leave the meeting feeling defensive and frustrated. There are a handful of phrases, which although sometimes well-meaning, are like nails on the chalkboard to the average teacher. Here are some of those things to avoid when talking to your child's teacher, and what to try instead to build a cooperative relationship centered on solutions and respect:

> "My child will be out for a week on a family vacation starting tomorrow. Can you please put together a packet of work for him to do, so he doesn't miss anything important

81

or fall behind?" Besides the obvious imposition on the teacher to get materials ready in advance on short notice, this request suggests that all the teaching and learning for the week can be consolidated down to a packet. It implies it's really not necessary for him to be there for the teaching, because he can just catch up on his own. Teachers spend a lot of time and energy preparing meaningful lessons and activities, and it is impossible to be gone for an entire week and not miss anything important. Instead, if your child has to be out during regular instructional time, inform the teacher he will be gone, and let her know you understand it is your child's responsibility to make up any work missed for credit. Make it clear you are more than willing to help him catch up on important things they will undoubtedly be missing. This communicates to the teacher that you understand how hard they work to provide meaningful lessons, and that it is not possible to get all the important stuff while gone. It also correctly places the responsibility with your child for their own work and learning.

"Why did you give my child this grade?" This can send the message you believe your child's grades are the teacher's responsibility instead of your child's. Teachers don't just arbitrarily give grades. Students earn them through what they have done or not done, and how they've demonstrated mastery or a lack thereof. Grades are indicators of those things and a summary of progress, not trophies or punishments. Instead try, "I am concerned about my child's grade in. . . I would like to set up a time to talk to you about what he might be having trouble with, and how he can improve that grade for next time." If your child is old enough, definitely in the middle school and high school years, you should talk to him first about what he may not have done or what he might be having a hard time with. Next, encourage him to talk to the teacher himself to get extra help, or about how and if he can improve the grade. Then you can have a follow up conversation with the teacher after your child has first taken responsibility for his own academic success.

"I need you to send home some extra credit for my daughter to improve her math grade." As a teacher my first thought with requests like this is usually, "Well, she should have done the regular credit." Extra credit is just that—something extra. It's extra work for teachers to put together and assign extra credit assignments, and it should be a way for students to go above and beyond. If a child has not done the regularly assigned work, extra credit is not an acceptable way to improve the poor grade earned by not doing that work. When coming up on grade deadlines, parents often panic because their child's grades are lower than expected and think forcing her to do a bunch of extra credit will help. If grades are lower than expected, often it is due to many missing assignments or poor test and project performance. So instead, work with the teacher on a plan to provide students some extra help in areas they are struggling with, or support to consistently turn assignments in on time and for full credit.

"I think my child's acting out because he's bored in your class." What you're really communicating to the teacher is that your child's behavior is not his own responsibility, but the teacher's. It's actually making an excuse for poor behavior on your child's part. Essentially, wording it this way is calling the teacher and her lessons boring and solely blaming those things for your child's misbehavior, putting the teacher on the defensive. If you really believe your child is not being engaged and challenged, stay away from insulting generalizations and instead focus on specifics. For example: if Henry is acting out in math class, and you believe it's because he truly is bored say something like, "Henry seems to have all his basic facts mastered, could we give him something more challenging during that review time?" This gives the teacher an opportunity to confirm or deny whether he does indeed have his facts mastered, and to provide a challenge for him without her personality and teaching methods being questioned or used as an excuse for inappropriate behavior.

"My child said she. . . (did turn in that assignment, you didn't give her enough time, you don't like her, etc.)" Sometimes kids lie, and it's possible that what your child is telling you about school or their teacher isn't true. These kinds of accusations assume the professional educator in the situation has more of a reason to lie to you or is less responsible than your kid. It is pitting the word of an adult against a child. Who has more of an incentive to lie to you in this scenario—the teacher who also wishes your child would have just turned in the assignment, making everyone's lives easier, or the child who will not be able to go to the sleepover this weekend if their work is not done and their grades are not acceptable? The teacher will not be the one grounded when the truth is found out. Can we agree that, as the adults in the situation, I won't automatically believe everything your child comes to school and tells me about home, if you won't automatically believe everything your child comes home to tell you about school? Instead of laying out what your child has said and forcing the teacher to take up the defensive in explaining her side of the story, start with an open ended question that assumes the teacher has some valuable insight into the problem. You might say, "Kelly seems to have trouble turning in her assignments on time, what are you seeing?" You may be surprised at what's actually going on that even your well-behaved, normally responsible child wants to keep from you.

A Communication Confession

I have to be honest and tell you that parent/teacher communication has not always been my strength as a teacher. I've definitely learned some lessons the hard way. As a new teacher I tended to focus only on my students, but didn't really get to know their families. I assumed no news from home was good news, and generally steered clear of dealing with parents as much as possible. When I first started teaching, I was young and insecure, and conversations with parents left me feeling intimidated and defensive. This was not the parents' fault however. I was overwhelmed and didn't always have the answers they were looking for, so I hid. I avoided phone calls and kept conversations to a minimum, instead of finding the answers and working it out together. I didn't trust myself as an expert in what I was doing yet, and wanted everyone to leave me alone until I figured it out. I avoided communicating with parents unless absolutely necessary because every time I talked to them, the words came out wrong, and I felt like I'd offended them. But I needed to drop my defense mechanisms and excuses and learn to communicate with the most important partners I had in educating my students.

What I want you to know is that, just like parents, teachers have a really hard job, and we care deeply about it and your children. Just like parenting, teaching is a matter of trial and error sometimes. Just like you, we make mistakes, and hurt feelings, and drop the ball sometimes. Just like you, we end any given day fully aware of our failures and shortcomings. We're both worn out, and figuring it out. So let's sit down, have a talk, and work on this thing together. Let's give each other space to ask questions and give honest feedback. We don't have to have all the solutions, we just need to be willing to work together to find them.

"Effective two way parent/teacher communication is essential to student success."

Lynda Patterson, Kindergarten Teacher

"The transformative nature of communication can ignite passion and offer new perspectives within the field of education. When communication is used to build and transform relationships, we all become advocates of education, and the possibilities for our students are endless."

Jessica Kamrath, High School
English/Communication Teacher.

CHAPTER SIX: *FUNDRAISERS, VOLUNTEERS, AND WHAT TEACHERS REALLY WANT HELP WITH*

I first met Grandma Deb on Meet the Teacher Night before school even began for the year. She was the grandmother of one of my third grade students and came with a shock of spiky red hair and plenty of opinions. She informed me she would be volunteering a lot in the classroom because she was always available. The first week of school she brought me a huge bin full of teaching supplies like post-it notes and pencils and insistently reminded me she was always available to help with whatever I needed.

At first I thought I had hit the volunteer jackpot. I assured her repeatedly I would get a schedule together and let her know when I could use her help. But soon I realized what "always available" really meant. It meant she was retired and would show up whenever she felt like it, because she was always available. She would walk in to drop something off that she'd been working on for me and then take it upon herself to reorganize my bookshelves—because she was always available. She stayed way past the time it took her to help me with a given task, just wanting to chat—because she was always available. One day I returned to my classroom after dropping the kids off at P.E. to find she had let herself into the room. She was sitting at my desk with her purse and lunch spread out on my things, writing her granddaughter a note on my personal stationary because she was—always available.

Things were getting a little out of hand, so I told her we really needed to stick to the regularly scheduled time for her to come in. She was not happy about that. I also found she didn't have much interest in doing the things I actually needed help with, but more interest in doing what she felt needed to be done. She didn't honestly have much respect for routines, or procedures, or even me for that matter.

Despite having a set time, she emailed me one day to tell me she'd be coming at a different time. That day, we were doing some end of quarter testing, and I was frustrated that she wasn't getting the hint. But I emailed her back and politely explained I would set some things aside for her to work on from home. I had a game which needed to be cut apart and assembled, so I left it with the front office for her to pick up during that time. That way, she wouldn't disturb the testing.

After finishing up the test and dropping my students off at lunch, I was returning to my classroom, weighed down with stacks from the copy machine and books from the library. I had since learned the lesson to lock my classroom door when I wasn't going to be in there, but when I turned the corner, I saw Grandma Deb standing at my door with her hand on her hip.

She thrust the game toward me and said, "I don't really want to do this. I want to be working with the kids, so I'm just going to wait until they get back from lunch."

I was now officially irritated, and the stack was getting heavy. So I simply said, "You know what Deb? I totally appreciate your willingness to help. But if you don't want to do what I could really use help with, then you don't have to come in anymore. I totally understand."

She huffed off and proceeded to inform the receptionist in the front office that I was a "very unfriendly woman," and that was the end of Grandma Deb volunteering for me.

This is the opposite of what volunteering in the classroom should look like. Instead of creating less work for me, it created more. I was constantly trying to find something for her to do to keep her busy and out of my bookshelves. Instead of taking something off of my plate, allowing me more time for teaching and investing in the students, it added something to my plate, a big old helping of Grandma Deb to contend with every day. Instead of being an extra set of hands to work with the kids, she actually was more like an extra kid to work with.

I am positive that Deb had good intentions. She thought she was being helpful, and she wanted to be involved in her grandchild's education. However she didn't realize she was adding to my stress level instead of helping with it.

I want you to know what we teachers could really use help your help with. I want to give you some practical suggestions for volunteering, and ways to be involved even if you can't come into the classroom.

Taking Something Off the Plate

Teachers have full plates. Nobody would argue that, even the people who mistakenly believe we only work nine months out of the year. Anybody who has spent even one hour with one child knows that to keep 20-30 kids at a time alive, let alone educated, is no simple task. Time and energy are our most precious resources as educators, and volunteering can help with both of those limited reserves. The goal of volunteering should be to take something off of teachers' plates, and never to add something to those already full plates.

Unfortunately, and even with the best of intentions, the opposite often happens in the world of parent volunteers in the classroom. Parents and family members sometimes think volunteering is about spending time with their child, making school more fun, or being on the inside track of what's going on during the school day. In my experience, parents who volunteer for those reasons tend to add to a teacher's workload and miss an opportunity to be truly helpful.

On the other hand, when parents volunteer to give the teacher more time for planning and teaching, to be an extra set of hands and eyes during activities requiring more supervision, or to provide needed resources to schools and classrooms on limited budgets, the results can be wonderful. Their help can improve the educational opportunities for their child as well as create a cooperative community. Here are some things to keep in mind to when volunteering in the classroom:

> Arrive on time, and leave on time. A typical school day is very schedule and routine oriented. If you are scheduled to volunteer at a certain time, be there at that time. Being early is not helpful in this situation, since the teacher more than likely has a different activity going on until your scheduled time. Being late also throws things off since she may be counting on you to lead an activity or work with students. Also, be sure to leave on time. It is tempting to plop down on a pint-sized chair and just take it all in, but extra adults in the classroom can be distracting for both the students and teacher.

> Be willing to help with the less than glamorous tasks. Fundraisers, field trips, and classroom parties are not the only ways to help out at school. Sometimes what teachers need help with most are the tedious, time-consuming tasks which take us away from time to plan meaningful lessons

and teach. Offering to label books for the classroom library, cut out laminated games to be used in the classroom, or prepare materials for an art project or science experiment are sometimes the most appreciated tasks, even if they're done from home.

Follow the teacher's lead. As it relates to interacting with students, volunteers are really expected to meet the same expectations as employees. Dress and talk appropriately for working with children. Often a teacher has very specific directions about how she would like things done, and it is for a reason. Remember she is the boss of the classroom, and has worked very hard to lay the foundation of expectations for the class. Never undermine the teacher or try to take charge. If the adults in the classroom are on the same page, the students receive a consistent message and you are helping to maintain order in a positive learning environment. If you do have a concern, discuss it privately with the teacher afterwards.

Share your strengths. Tell the teacher about areas of interest and expertise for you. Don't make the mistake of thinking that because you aren't great with large groups of kids or heading up big events, there is no place for you to help out in your child's education. There are many different areas where teachers would love to put your talents and passions to good use. If you are an artist, coming in to share an art lesson to go along with a particular topic, or creating a visual aid of some sort for a unit would be fabulous. If you are a bit shy but love books, volunteer to read one-on-one with children who might need some extra help reading. If you have great organizational skills, offer to help in the details of an event or project. If you are a carpenter, offer to build a bookshelf. If you are a lion tamer. . . you get the picture.

Help Should Be Helpful

At the beginning of each school year, I would send home an inventory for parents interested in volunteering to fill out. Maybe you've seen something similar from your child's school. It usually included a list of available times and the different activities I needed help with in the classroom. I also included things that parents could do from home to help out too. I chose specific things for this list because they were areas where I knew I would be needing help. I also knew I could easily accommodate extra helpers in those areas without creating more work for myself.

Sometimes it was easier because of time constraints or other restrictions to do something myself, than to explain to someone else how to do it. I would even have to occasionally re-do things done incorrectly or sloppily by certain volunteers. I found that not all help was helpful. The best volunteers were always the type who followed instructions, but could also take initiative to step in where needed without being pushy.

When I taught English language learners, a little girl named Ella joined us a couple of months into the school year. Her family had temporarily moved from Denmark to the U.S. for her Dad's job. Her mom, who was a graphic designer, worked mostly from home, and had a very flexible schedule. So she asked (in her friendly Danish accent) if she could come in once a week to help out with anything I needed.

This was new to me. It was only my second year teaching, and the first time I had a regular parent volunteer. The parents of my students were very involved with their kids and cared deeply about education, but usually the language barrier and jobs just didn't allow many of them the opportunity to volunteer other than an occasional field trip. I was admittedly intimidated at the idea of a parent watching my every move and maybe discovering that I didn't always know what I was doing. But, I had sixteen boys and five girls that year and welcomed the extra set of eyes and hands to deal with my active class.

My worries were unfounded. Ella's mom was such a big help. She willingly hung artwork for me, checked folders, and helped supervise during centers. She was great with the kids, and an extra set of hands to lovingly open snacks, clean up spilled glitter, and redirect wandering little feet. I rarely had to ask her to do anything. She just quietly took initiative where she could see help was needed. I appreciated her help so much, and was disappointed when they moved back to Denmark toward the end of the year.

Ella's mom seamlessly blended into our routines to support student learning and well-being. Unfortunately though, sometimes volunteers misunderstand the goal of helping out. Volunteering is not just about parents hanging out with their kids. Sometimes parents have a day off and want to spend it with their child, so they volunteer to come in and just end up hanging out right next to their kid's desk.

Or they volunteer to chaperone a field trip but their main reason for volunteering is to create photo opportunities for cute selfies of them with their child on the bus. These are the parents who may take their small group around the zoo on a field trip, go against all teacher requests, and buy them all sorts of ice cream and those alligator puppet-on-a-stick souvenirs from the gift shop. Then they return to the bus 20 minutes late, because they were having so much fun on the playground. On behalf of all teachers, I beg of you not to be that parent.

While spending time and creating memories with your child are definitely benefits to volunteering, try to keep in mind the bigger picture of getting involved and helping out. The purpose of volunteering is to support the school and classroom environment to create better opportunities for your child and all of the other students.

There Are Limits

The process to volunteer at your child's school may seem daunting. Often there is a sign-in process with ID required, a badge to wear, and even a background check to be completed and kept on file for anyone in direct contact with students. These policies can seem unfriendly, but many of these school rules are really designed to protect your child. Although an open door approach seems ideal to create community, it isn't always possible. As much as I would have loved for (some) of my students' parents to be able to drop in whenever they wanted, the school has a right and a responsibility to keep track of the people in the building. Certain laws and safety measures are necessary with so many children in the school's care.

Be aware, there are also very strict laws concerning student confidentiality. Parent volunteers are not entitled to specific records or information about other students. This is especially important when working directly with groups or individual students. The teacher will assign you an activity to do with them based on the information she has, but she cannot share specific information about an individual student with you just because you are working with that child. Similarly, behaviors you witness while in the classroom, conversations you overhear, or confidential matters and documents to which you have access to as a volunteer should remain confidential.

ERICA LADD

Fundraisers That Actually Raise Useful Funds

I have found that parents of my students, and even my own
family members, are shocked at what isn't provided by the school
and what teachers typically spend their own money on. If I only
used what was provided by my school I would have no classroom
decorations, informational posters, pocket charts, games, rugs, art
supplies, pencil sharpeners, or a classroom library. Many people
don't realize that depending on the school and the district, bare
bones are usually the only things provided due to limited budgets.
Every school is a little different, but usually there are few things like
text books, desks, a bookshelf, a filing cabinet, and if we're lucky,
copy paper provided by the school. The rest of what you see in a
teacher's classroom has likely been bought with his or her own
money or been donated from another teacher. Begging at Home
Depot for materials and dumpster diving for old shelving behind
retail stores is also considered normal practice. Moving classrooms
is truly like moving houses because of all our personal belongings.
Teachers tend to struggle with hoarder-like tendencies in finding
and keeping things to provide a fully furnished, functional, creative
space for our students. In my opinion, a great fundraiser should
raise funds to directly impact the students in their classrooms by
offsetting some of these costs.

The Parent Teacher Organization in a school where I taught
did a great job with raising funds to actually be used in the
classroom. Their biggest fundraiser of the year was the annual fall

98

carnival. They paid attention to what teachers really needed, which was money for classroom materials. While it was a lot of work for the entire staff and parent volunteers, it was structured to give teachers an incentive to help out and made for a great event. Each grade level was responsible for one or two booths with games, food, or other activities. The teachers decided what they wanted to do and then manned their own booths. The money raised from their booths was split directly among the teachers in the grade level to put to use in their classrooms. The better our booths did, the more money we had to put towards classroom supplies like games, books, and even furniture. After the carnival, we simply hung on to our receipts and turned them in to the PTO for reimbursement on classroom related items. Running a fundraiser this way had two positive effects. It helped to foster school spirit and a sense of community around a family friendly event, and it allowed teachers to use their own creativity to raise funds which actually went toward things they needed.

Another thoughtful thing the PTO did was to use money raised through other fundraisers throughout the year to throw a Back to School Luncheon for teachers. It was so nice to have one less meal to think about during busy hours spent in meetings and preparing our classrooms to welcome our new students. They then used the luncheon to explain what they had planned for the year, and get feedback from us about our needs. At the end of the lunch they gave us each a big tote bag full of essentials like tissues, pencils, construction paper, paper clips, hand sanitizer, etc. It was a great way to invite teachers to partner with the volunteers on the PTO in events happening in the school community. At the same time, it showed appreciation for the teachers' hard work by feeding them, and sending them on their way with some goodies.

Fundraisers are one of the main ways parents get involved, but when they're not done well, fundraisers really create a lot of extra work teachers and take away from teaching and learning. This is changing in many schools, but if your child's school does a lot of selling gift wrap or frozen desserts and cookie dough, teachers probably are not thrilled. These types of fundraisers tend to require lots of money collecting, and reminding from teachers to raise funds which they may never see in the classroom.

Good alternatives to fundraiser sales would be things like Read-a-Thons that provide gift cards to add to the library of the classroom that raises the most money. A Fun Run where students are sponsored, but a parent volunteer from each classroom is the coach who does all of the organizing is also a great idea.

You Don't Have to Volunteer to Be Involved

Volunteering is one way to be involved, but it's not the only way. We know students whose parents are involved in their education have better success academically and socially at school, but that does not mean you need to be the PTO president. In fact there are easier, less time consuming ways to be involved—to show your children you value education, want them to succeed, and provide support for them. Here a just a few ideas:

Meet basic needs. This might seem like an obvious one, but just making sure your children consistently have enough sleep, a good breakfast, and clean clothes is so important and shouldn't be underestimated.

Raise readers. If I could pick the most valuable thing you can do to support your child's education, this would be it. Reading is such a foundational skill to most other learning, and that doesn't mean you need to teach your children to read. Just read to them at all different times, any kind of story, in any language. Let them read to you. Even if it's just letting them retell a story by looking at the pictures or from memorization, it's an important pre-reading skill. Have books accessible all over the house. Put favorite bedtime stories in their bedrooms, some in the seat back pocket of the car, and even some in the kitchen for them to look at independently while you make dinner. Let them see you reading. Read books, your e-reader, magazines, newspapers, or comic books. Model what readers do, and take time to read for yourself. Talk about things you've read together. When they ask you what you're reading, tell them. Talk about the stories you read with them. Ask them questions about the book. Give books as gifts and let them pick out books as rewards. Make books a positive thing, never a punishment. Make trips to libraries and book stores a regular, fun activity (See Chapter 9).

Set high expectations. This doesn't mean that you expect them to be a rock star at everything. It means you expect them to try their best academically and behaviorally at school, and that you will hold them accountable for both (See Chapter 3).

Communicate with teachers. Let them know when you notice a difficulty your child is having. Ask the teachers how they're doing. Make every effort to attend school activities and conferences. It sends a message to your child and the school that you care about what's happening in your child's education (See Chapter 5).

Make school a priority. Send a message that school matters by making it a priority. Create a routine and an organized area for homework and other school related things like backpacks and checking papers in your home. Make it clear that school comes before other activities, and try not to pull them out of school frequently.

A Volunteer's Point of View

In the process of writing this book, I frequently visited schools to volunteer with some of my teacher friends. Jenny teaches kindergarten, and one day I spent some time with small groups of her students to create a bat art project the week before Halloween. It showed me a few things from a volunteer's perspective, which I thought I would share with you as tips for a successful volunteering experience.

First of all, when working with kids, time always moves faster than you think it will. I had groups of four students at a time outside with me at a picnic table making their bats. 15 minutes is not enough time to have a chat, or leisurely allow kids to trace and cut out a head, wings, a mouth, and glue on googly eyes and a silly pipe cleaner bowtie that will not stick. You are there to assist in moving things along, a fact I was reminded of when the timer went off to rotate stations, and most of my kids unfortunately had only half a bat finished. If you're asked to work with a group of kids, it is because they will need assistance to stay on track. The younger they are, the more assistance they will generally need.

Dress appropriately and comfortably. I was reminded of how much bending and reaching one does when wrangling groups of five-year-olds. You might be on the floor, outside in the sun, and getting glue, paint, or snot on you. So this is not the time to wear anything you spent more than $14.99 on. Also, mind the gap. Low cut and low rise are not appropriate for the stooping and squatting necessary when working with kids. Plan footwear wisely. Heels always seem like a great idea, until you've chased a fly-away art project across the playground on a breezy day.

Wash your hands frequently. I kid you not: I was sneezed and coughed on by one in four children during the hour and a half I was there. I actually counted, because I couldn't believe that in every single group of children I worked with, there was one child who managed to share germs with me. My rule as a teacher, which I'm quickly remembering as a volunteer, was to wash my hands last thing before I leave the classroom, first thing when I walk in the door at home, and definitely before eating anything.

Keep a close eye. Remember your first and most important job, especially with little ones, is to make sure everyone is safe and accounted for. I turned my head for five seconds to set a bat on a neighboring table to dry, and turned back around just in time to catch one little guy winding up with a pair of scissors to chuck it across the table at a friend who was asking to use them.

"Absolutely not," I told him with big eyes. He knew. (As a side note, just make sure they each have their own materials. Sharing with kindergarteners when you're trying to get something done efficiently is no good.)

Get lots of sleep the night before. I was exhausted when I got home because I had not gone to bed early enough. By the time I got home the coffee had worn off, and I needed a nap. You will be amazed at what that kind of constant vigilance can do to your energy levels.

Volunteer Vulnerability

Finally, I want you to know we desperately need your help, even though it's difficult to ask for or manage at times. Teachers can be very insecure individuals. It can be terrifying to invite parents into our classrooms to watch us teach your children, the most precious people on the planet to you. We really want help with the little organizational tasks we just don't have time for, but we worry you'll think we're disorganized. We wonder if you'll think we're doing a good job. We wonder if you'll see the bags under our eyes, or remember that we wore the same dress pants yesterday. We wonder if you'll notice how brilliant and creative our lesson was, or if you'll catch us at our worst, most impatient moment of the day. But, the bottom line is we want and need your help. Just please don't rearrange our bookshelves without asking first.

"With your help and concern, we can give your child the most authentic education. Balancing involvement and support, together we can ensure success."

Tara Dunn, *Fifth Grade Teacher*

"Teachers are creatures of habit and routine. Establishing practices and procedures takes a lot of time and effort, and in very little time it can all be undone. I think the effective use of volunteers is the result of careful planning and realistic expectations from both the teacher and parent."

Brigid Johannes, Second Grade Teacher

CHAPTER SEVEN: *CLOROX WIPES, A TYPICAL DAY, AND WHY TEACHERS NEED A SUMMER BREAK*

I stood in the hall monitoring my third grade students as they went in and out for a class bathroom break. It was one of those necessary parts of the day that has nothing to do with teaching, but falls under the 'other duties' category. I didn't mind too much, because it was a chance for all of us to get out of the classroom, stretch our legs, and take a small break. After a few minutes, Travis came out of the bathroom with a very concerned look on his face. I had learned over the years that a student coming out of the bathroom with a concerned look on his face was never a good sign. He motioned he had a secret to tell me—an even worse sign.

I bent down so he could whisper in my ear, "Uh…Mrs. Ladd…I went in the stall to. . . ya know. . . use it. And there was. . . um. . . it's. . . there was some. . . brown business. . . all over the stall."

My eyes got big, and I was horrified but stifling laughter as I said very seriously, "Oh. Goodness. That's a situation. Why don't you go use the other bathroom at the end of the hall, and then go to the office and tell Ms. Anna about it so we can get that cleaned up."

As he hurried off doing a bit of an urgent potty dance, he shouted down the hall behind him, "Oh great! Then I can kill two birds with one stone, because Ms. Anna is a Dallas Cowboys fan, and I've been meaning to tell her that I too am a fan of the Cowboys." I was glad he'd found a silver lining in the brown business of life that day.

I would like to be able to tell you this was the only time I encountered such brown business while teaching, but that would be sadly untrue. When teaching kindergarten one year, I had a particularly mischievous little student. Matthew was all huge brown eyes and charming smiles. (Why are the naughtiest kids usually the cutest?) Unfortunately, the bathroom was one of his favorite places to make mischief.

One day during a class bathroom break, another student, Mario, came running out of the bathroom quite upset. Mario was very new to English and tried his best to convey to me what had happened, but it came out as, "Matthew! Matthew. . . he. . . he. . . he. . . floor!" while pointing toward the bathroom.

I quickly started to piece it together and knew that nothing involving Matthew, a bathroom, and a floor could be good. I immediately went to the door of the bathroom, and told Matthew to come out of there in no uncertain terms. He shuffled out into the hallway, hanging his head, and refusing to look at me.

"What happened?" I asked him. He just shook his head. I tried again with an even firmer voice, "Matthew, tell me what happened."

Now he was crying, not because he felt bad, but because he knew there was no escaping.

He looked up at me eventually with tears filling those big brown eyes, and blurted out, "I poofed on da floor! I poofed on da floor."

There are just no words for that occasion when a child admits to pulling down their pants, and "poofing" on the bathroom floor intentionally. Nothing throws a wrench in your day like calming down a giggly group of boys who've just witnessed a poofing. Then there's the conversation in the hallway with the principal, alternating between utter despair and fits of laughter as you try to determine whether or not said "poofing" was intentional, and decide together what an acceptable consequence should be.

No college course in my teacher preparation covered that one. When's the last time someone poofed on the floor at your place of employment? Everyone's job has its inherent difficulties, but I would be willing to bet it's been a long time since anyone poofed on the floor just for fun. These are the kinds of antics teachers are dealing with here on a daily basis.

Teaching is so much more than reading, writing, and arithmetic. In fact, I think at least half the day is spent as a teacher

on troubleshooting and other duties, which have nothing to do
with academics whatsoever. When you are with 20-30+ children
for eight hours a day, other things are bound to come up, and even
take precedence over the math lesson at hand. Allow me to
continue to paint you a picture of a day in the life of your average
elementary teacher. For grins and giggles, and some insight into
what this job actually entails, I'm going to show you why teachers
really do need a summer break.

I've chosen to describe an ordinary day in the teaching world.
I can't even begin to describe a day like Halloween or the day
before Christmas Break, for which I'd rather hide under the covers
and call a substitute teacher (but I don't because that constitutes
cruelty to subs). I've also intentionally chosen to not describe a
typical day in the life of a kindergarten teacher. That is a whole
other story, and no day is typical. Kindergarten is like the ocean,
it's absolutely beautiful, but you never turn your back on it, and
you could be in over your head before you realize what's
happening. So instead, here is a play-by-play of an average day
teaching second grade. . .

7:09 After hitting snooze too many times, I get ready, pack my
lunch, and fill the biggest travel mug I own with precious coffee for
the drive to work. I try to pretend it only takes 11 minutes to get to
work, and I can be there by 7:20. I'm mentally kicking myself,
because I know if I could manage to get up earlier and get to work
early, I would feel less rushed and more prepared every morning.

They told me I would become a morning person after a few years of teaching. They lied, and I'm not.

7:28 I actually get to work, and unload from the trunk my rolling suitcase of good intentions. It is filled with things I took home to catch up on and never did—papers I didn't grade, and projects I didn't prepare.

7:30 I juggle my coffee, suitcase, lunch, and purse while trying to unlock my classroom door. I immediately drop all my things right inside the door and turn my computer on to try to get ten minutes of work done before my colleagues start arriving and asking questions about the day. When my computer is fired up, I see an email from our principal about a mandatory staff meeting after school. Yippee. I also read five emails from parents. Two of them are confused about last night's math homework. One is concerned her daughter is being bullied on the playground, and wants me to make sure I'm watching at all times during recess. Another is emailing to tell me her son won't be in school for a week because his grandparents are in town. She wants me to get all work he will be missing to the office by lunch time that day so she can pick it up on her lunch break. The last one wants me to check the classroom, because her son hasn't brought his lunch box home all week. He says he lost it. I glance over at the shelf above the coat rack, and sure enough, there is a Spiderman lunchbox abandoned in the corner. I'm sure there are new life forms growing in it by now.

7:40 After sifting through emails, I glance at the clock and realize I only have five minutes left to get outside to my post for supervising morning drop off. I must decide between going to the bathroom and getting morning work up on the board for the students. I had a doctor's appointment the night before, so I had to jet right after school, and didn't get it ready. I choose morning work, not wanting children waiting for me to get something ready, because that's just asking for trouble. I know I can always open the door to my adjoining classroom, and ask the teacher next door to supervise for a second. I'll run to the bathroom while my kids are working. I'm amazed at how many times a day I have to choose between meeting my own basic physical needs and job requirements.

7:45 I grab my coffee (now lukewarm, but still caffeinated) and head out to morning duty, where I attempt to keep traffic moving as I open sticky car doors, grinning and greeting students. No one else seems to be a morning person either, because my friendly smile is not returned, and I am actually jealous of one first grader's Coach backpack as I help her out of her Escalade. My main job at this particular juncture is to keep cars flowing, to make sure no parent goes into road rage, and no student gets run over in the cluster crisis that is the morning traffic pattern. What a great way to start the day.

7:55 The morning bell rings signaling the kids to line up, and I head around the back of the school to greet my class. They are mostly lined up and ready to start the day, with the exception of a few. I notice one child crying because she forgot her library books. Another is wearing a parka, gloves, hat, and scarf. It's November in Arizona, but after the brutal summer, I guess 67 degrees feels like winter. A third child is twirling around in oblivious circles, until I interrupt her, and she staggers off dizzy to join the line. I'm pretty sure she has forgotten to take her medication today.

8:00 We've all made it inside. The students are hanging up backpacks and putting their folders in the designated basket for me. I head over to my desk to enter morning attendance into the computer. I have a line on the floor made from colorful duct tape, which separates my desk area from the rest of the classroom. I call the designated area The Zone of Teacherness, and students know they may not touch things on my desk and shelves, or even cross the line unless they are invited to do so. They also know I am taking attendance and handling other administrative things right away, and they should go about their own business of starting the day unless they have an emergency. But, that doesn't stop two of them from lining up and staring at me sheepishly from behind the duct tape line. I ask calmly, "Is this an emergency?" They both shake their heads no, so I wave goodbye and remind them to sit down and raise their hands if they need to tell me something. I assure them I will be with them in just a minute. This may seem harsh, but I learned the hard way that if you don't have some sort of system like this in place, you will be bum-rushed by at least 15 children every morning who have urgent news for you. By urgent I mean they want to tell you their cat is going to the vet today, or their uncle is visiting from Minnesota, all of which are important to them and should be heard, but are not necessary for me to know right that instant.

8:10 While the students settle in and start their morning work on the board, I go through their folders to check homework and make sure there are no parent notes, permission slips, or book orders to deal with. In the meantime, I notice Braydon hacking ceaselessly into his morning work notebook. I send him to the nurse, not wanting other students (or myself) to catch the apparent plague he has brought with him. The nurse calls down to my room to ask if someone can bring his things down for him, because he has a fever of 102 and will be going home. Wonderful. Enter Clorox wipes for the first time that day in an attempt to disinfect everything Braydon's touched in his short time in the classroom.

8:20 The remaining students and I go over the morning work and begin Reading Stations. I am proud and grinning to myself because at this point in the year, reading is a well-oiled machine. They are quietly working at their stations, for the most part, rotating to the next one with little disturbance, and I am really making progress with the group at my reading table until . . . the fire alarm goes off! My student who has autism screams and covers her ears until we are outside. We line up on the far end of the playground, and I count students. I'm one short. How could that be? I think back to attendance and everyone was here today. I count again. I'm still missing one, and feeling panicky until I finally ask the kids, "Who's missing?" "Braydon," one says. "He went home sick remember?"

Oh yeah. Phew.

9:15 We get settled back into the classroom after the fire drill. The distraction is a bit much for my twirler from earlier that morning who begins taking everything out of her crayon box and reorganizing it instead of doing her work. Other than her, mostly everyone goes back to work. We get through the rest of reading time successfully. I tell students to meet me at the carpet for writing, while I ask the teacher's assistant (a classroom job for a student) to pass out whiteboards and markers for our mini lesson on adding suffixes to words. On the way to the carpet, I stop at my desk where I see a new email from a parent telling me they will be dropping off a cake for McKayla's birthday after lunch. A whole cake, and she wants to know if I have forks and plates to serve it. Mercy. I scribble "cake" on a sticky note so I remember to stop in the break room to see if I can scrounge up some forks and plates later. I head over to the carpet to see kids with no whiteboards. "Who's my teacher's assistant this week? Why doesn't anybody have whiteboards?" "It's Braydon, he went home sick, remember?" Katie speaks up. "Oh yeah," I remember again.

"Katie can you pass them out for me then?"

10:30 It's time for Writer's Workshop. This truly is one of my favorite times of the day. It starts with a ten minute mini lesson on a specific skill or topic to pay attention to in their writing for the day, and then students work independently on pieces of writing while I confer individually with them. Classical music plays in the background, and it is truly peaceful until . . . Jack runs to the garbage can to vomit and just barely makes it. I am both revolted and grateful that he didn't puke on his desk or anywhere near me, as I am a joiner. I have made it abundantly clear to my students: if they feel like they need to be sick, they do not come tell me about it or ask to go to the bathroom. I've drilled it into them to just go quickly to the nearest garbage can. If they come tell me, they might puke on me. I assure them I will figure it out when I see them at the trash can, and won't need an explanation. Kids are also not great at planning ahead, so trying to rush to make it to the bathroom usually results in a pile of that sawdust stuff they sprinkle on puke in the middle of the hallway. Jack hadn't interrupted once during the mini lesson, and stayed in his seat the entire workshop time, so I should have known something was wrong. On that appetizing note, it's lunchtime, and time for more Clorox wipes to disinfect Jack's desk.

12:00 After getting Jack and his trash can of grossness hurried along to the nurse, I absentmindedly tell everyone to get ready for lunch. In my haste, I forget that a simple statement like, "Get ready for lunch," means all 27 second graders will rush toward the single coat rack in the classroom and crowd into the 12 square feet of space to grab their lunches. I immediately regret not sending them up a few at a time. Oh well, at this point we're already down from 35 to 30 minutes to eat, so we're just going to roll with it. Despite Brian who realizes he forgot his lunch, and Dallas who can't remember if he needs to get a hot lunch or if his mom is bringing him one, we eventually make it to the cafeteria, where I am relieved to drop them off. Lunch means a break for me to wolf down some food and breathe. I have 25 minutes left to microwave last night's pasta leftovers in the break room while making a quick copy for math that afternoon. Making a copy reminds me of the parent request to have all of her child's work at the front office to be picked up by lunch time. Yeah, that's not happening. I quickly scan the break room for plastic cutlery for the birthday cake. There is none, so I rush back to my classroom to eat my soggy leftovers with the remaining ten minutes of lunch. My mouth is full when two moms walk in my classroom door. One is holding a sheet cake and the other is standing with her hands on her hips and confusion on her face about why her son's work is not waiting for her to pick up in the office. With my mouth full of baked ziti, I have to explain to both of them why I cannot satisfy their last minute requests.

12:35 I meet the students on the playground to pick them up after lunch recess. They quickly get in a straighter line when they see me

coming. I smile and congratulate myself on what a great job I have
done to instill high expectations, until I get closer and three
children come running up to tattle about three different recess
offenses. Two other children at the front of the line are pushing
and shoving over whose turn it is to be line leader. Another is hot,
another is thirsty, and the twirler is spinning around with her lunch
box extended, completely oblivious to the fact that it's time to line
up. While listening to the various grievances and directing my
ballerina back into line, I do a quick head count and notice one is
missing. I know Jack threw up and went home, but I'm still missing
one. I start to ask, "Who's miss . . ." and before I can even finish
the question about 17 children yell back, "Braydon!" Oh yeah. I
close my eyes and take a deep breath before I attempt crowd
control. We eventually make it back inside with everyone
accounted for.

12:40 Silent Reading— Hands down my favorite time of the day
for obvious reasons.

1:00 Math starts out with a daily warm up of review activities on
the interactive white board. This expensive piece of technology can
be awesome, but is more frequently not working and a thorn in my
side. Today is no exception since it is on the fritz, so the slide with
the problems for students to do is not available. This is one of those
many moments in a teacher's day where winging it becomes
necessary. No matter how prepared you are, things always come

up and you need a Plan B at the ready, or you will have mutiny on your hands in a heartbeat. Although the exercises on the computer would have been much more exciting, with interactive coins to count change and a clock to manipulate and show times, I quickly write a few review problems on the regular old whiteboard. We move on.

2:00 It's mercifully time for a Special Class! These precious 35 minutes four times a week are my only prep periods, and are otherwise known as a time when teachers can at least use the bathroom while the students are in Art, Music, P.E., or Library. Today is P.E., so the changing into tennis shoes commences.

2:35 I pick up the kids from P.E., and we head back to the classroom for them to get their snacks. I grab a stack of papers to grade before we head outside for afternoon recess. I give one student a reminder before he heads off to play to keep his hands to himself, and refrain from tackling classmates this recess. I realize I forgot to grab a walkie talkie for the office to get a hold of us while we're outside, so I ask Katie to go to the office and get one before the secretary has to come out and give us a grumpy face again when she tries to reach us and can't. Just as I've finished grading the first paper on my stack, a student comes up in apparent agony. Like a wounded warrior being helped off the field of battle, he has a loyal companion on either side, practically holding him up. I would normally be concerned, but this is Kevin, a child with quite the flair for the dramatic. So I thank his companions for their concern and delivering him safely, and ask him to sit down next to me. I see his knee is skinned, but he immediately bends it, so I am certain that nothing is broken and he will live. Recess triage and seeing through some false tears is another one of any teacher's well-honed skills.

2:50 We head inside for Social Studies where we continue to work on our neighborhood map project. Some students are already finished, so they're creating a second map of an imaginary neighborhood they've designed. The perfectionists in the room are meticulously measuring everything to scale and drawing all their straight lines with a ruler or asking for another piece of paper because they've messed up again. The less than motivated cartographers in the group have scribbled a square for their house, a rectangle for the grocery store, and colored the rest of it green for the parks. My twirler is sharpening her colored pencil by whittling away at the lead with her scissors under her desk.

3:35 Pack up to go home. This takes at least 15 minutes, so I read a chapter from a book every day while kids are quietly packing up and joining me over at the carpet when they're ready. It's a great calm way to end the day. I love it, the kids love it, and we all remember why we love each other again. Most days I remember to also end the day with asking kids to tell me one thing they learned that day, but today I forget because we are interrupted three times in our peaceful reading of The Mouse and the Motorcycle. The first two times are the receptionist buzzing down through the intercom in my room to tell me kids are leaving early. The third time is an end of day announcement to the whole school reminding them about the annual Fall Carnival the next night. With that, I give up on reading and we line up to go home because, well, the carnival has been mentioned, and I have lost my audience . . .

3:50 I walk the kids to an exit on the opposite end of the school from our classroom. Don't ask me who decided that was the door we must dismiss from, but keeping all of them and their backpacks, projects, and lunch boxes in order and out the door together is a small miracle every day. Some kids head to the bus, some start walking home, some see their parents' cars right away, and then there are the leftovers. Almost every day there are one to four children left over whose parents are late, or whose older brother has not picked them up yet. So every day we wait a few extra minutes, and then do the walk of shame to the office where they will need to call someone to come pick them up.

4:08 The staff meeting which was called at the last minute is beginning in the library. So I use the two minutes I now have, to grab the first caffeinated beverage I can get my hands on, a notebook and something to write with, and rush to the library so I can get a spot to sit.

4:30 After the meeting, I head to a fellow second grade teacher's classroom to take a peek at a computer problem and plan out the next week. Afterwards, we end up rehashing the day over leftover Halloween candy, because sometimes you just need to talk to someone who understands.

6:30 I get back to my classroom, write the morning work up on the board for the next day, and try to return my classroom into some semblance of order, before dragging my suitcase of good intentions back to my car and finally heading home at 7:00.

A Teacher's Job

I recently asked a group of teachers to tell me just one thing they had done that very day which had nothing to do with teaching or academics. I received back varied responses, some of them quite entertaining and surprising. One kindergarten teacher had spent a good portion of that day lining up parent volunteers to come in, and organizing paperwork. Another kindergarten teacher had used duct tape and a paper clip to fix a student's shoe. A first grade teacher had donned her finest rainbow gear to participate in a dress-up day for Red Ribbon Week, while another first grade teacher had just been happy to find the top of her desk again. A common theme was also janitorial duties. One teacher had spent 45 minutes cleaning off all her desks with Clorox wipes, while another had used good old-fashioned elbow grease to scrape gum and boogers off of her fifth grade students' desks.

After the school day is done, and a teacher has played many roles, from educator to nurse to referee to janitor, they often take on other roles sometimes for little or no pay like coach, tutor, or committee member. Teachers work for free for hours after their required work day just to be ready for the next day. I hope this chapter has shed some light on the many aspects of a teacher's job description, which have nothing to do with her job title. The bottom line is, give a teacher a hug, and perhaps a pack of Clorox wipes. They probably need both.

"There are literally thousands of decisions teachers make each day. It is important that we support and trust teachers whether or not we agree with or understand every single decision."

Matt Rawley, Principal

CHAPTER EIGHT: *SPELLING, CHANGES, AND WHAT HAPPENED TO CURSIVE*

It was Friday morning, and like every Friday morning in second grade, we were starting off with a spelling test. I would slowly read words we had learned that week, and then use them in a sentence to test just how well my students had committed them to memory. Every Monday a list of words went home, and they were used in many different activities throughout the week.

The patterns in the words were studied, and then the students were tested on them every Friday. I was never really quite comfortable with the way we did this. I felt like we were authentically studying the words during the week, but the rote memory test at the end of the week we were assessing them with didn't feel as authentic. These two things didn't seem to jive, but parents expected a spelling test with a grade every week, so that's what we gave them.

One particular Friday, I discovered how little good this test was actually doing. Brad was at his desk struggling but pretending to look calm. He kept looking under his desk, again and again, but I couldn't figure out what he was looking for. Soon I figured out he had slipped his spelling list in between the top of his desk and the bar that supported the desktop. He was trying his best to be sly— sliding it out, and then back in, to see how to spell each word before writing it on his paper.

In other words, he was cheating. The teacher in me was ready to march over and catch him in the act, scolding and disciplining him accordingly. Then I looked closer at his face.

Brad was a great kid. He was well-liked by his classmates, and had a charming, sincere personality. But he struggled in school— with pretty much everything. He consistently gave his all, but school was tough for him.

To make matters worse, he had two much older sisters who added pressure with their great grades and school involvement. His parents had high expectations of him, and lately had been so pleased his spelling test grades were improving, because they had been working hard with him at home. Every night his homework folder was stuffed with extra spelling activities, at their request, and he was proud to show me how hard he was working. I applauded their effort, and I had been pleasantly surprised to see his scores improve too. Until today, that is.

My heart sank knowing this was probably the main reason for the dramatic improvement. He had figured out a way to beat the system. Knowing him, it wasn't about trying to get away with something but feeling successful, and making his parents and teacher proud. In that moment I really began to question the value of this testing system. Did it accurately reflect learning? Did it reward the wrong things? I began to wonder: if it was this easy to cheat on the test, what real learning was taking place? What were we even measuring? When I looked at Brad, I had to honestly ask myself: Were my spelling tests praising the kids who were already successful, and forcing the others just to cope?

Something I was deeply surprised about in teaching was the weight parents placed on spelling. They discouraged kids from spelling words inventively or phonetically, which is an important step in their development. They wanted to know what the spelling words for the week were right away. They studied with their kids all week and were very concerned with their grades on spelling tests. There was certainly nothing wrong with being involved or concerned about spelling. But I had to wonder what it was about spelling in particular that was so important to them.

You may notice your children are being taught much differently than you were in school. Frequently I get questions and comments like this from parents, "Why don't you teach _____ anymore?" or "I don't understand this new way of teaching _____?" "How will my child be graded in _____?" "Why do these spelling words seem easier than when I was in school/when her sister was in second grade/what she had last year?"

Growing up in school, things like grammar, penmanship, and spelling were some of the most emphasized aspects of my education. We were taught to focus on the mechanics and appearance of writing, more frequently and often before the actual ideas behind our writing.

But what good is great penmanship in writing a superficial letter? Why does spelling matter if your word choices are immature and insufficient at getting ideas across? These are some of the questions we are asking ourselves as educators, and we haven't always done a great job of including parents in this particular conversation. This conversation needs to be had about the changing educational needs and priorities and how to address those changes.

Spelling Isn't Everything

In my experience, most parents just want to know how their kid is doing in school. They want an overall answer. They want to be assured of a general OK-ness with their child and concrete suggestions to fix things that may be less than OK. This is completely understandable, but there are certain aspects of education that moms and dads tend to cling to more than others as a means to determining success. Spelling is definitely one of those things. I think those things are usually the most familiar to parents, because they are still often taught in a way that adults can relate to and remember from their own childhoods. Familiarity translates into parents feeling confident to help their children with those areas.

In addition to familiarity, there is definite nostalgia on the part of parents for "the good old days." The common phrase heard is "Well, I was taught that way, and I turned out just fine." Did you? Did everyone? Who was left out? Who hates school and learning now? What other supports did you have at home? What strengths of yours were encouraged while weaknesses in others were made greater?

The problem is, while some teachers are still teaching things like back in the "good old days," a lot has changed in education since parents and teachers were in school themselves. Families look much different, and kids are coming to school with different experiences. The role that teachers and schools now play in the life of a child has increased. Students are also expected to know different things as a part of a changing world. Nobody likes change. We want things to stay the same, so we just keep doing things the way they've always been done. However, I'm sure you've noticed that things always do change, and nothing stays the same. Change is natural and inevitable. Families have changed, neighborhoods have changed, the whole economy has changed, and it would be silly to think that education is not affected by those changes, or that it shouldn't adjust accordingly. For better or worse, change is a part of education because it is a part of every other aspect of life. Not all changes are good ones, but we need to adjust nevertheless to meet new needs.

I can certainly understand the desire to keep doing things the way they've always been done, because beyond familiarity and nostalgia, it's often just easier. It continues to be tempting as a teacher to teach spelling words by copying a list out of the teacher's manual, sending that list home, asking students to memorize it, and then testing them on it every Friday. It's much easier than using relevant words to the students, teaching spelling as a more complex word study involving word parts and their meanings, or expecting students to use the words they've learned correctly. But, memorization is one of the lowest forms of learning.

According to Bloom's Taxonomy, the standard for classifying learning objectives in the world of education, remembering or recalling previously learned information is only the most basic level of understanding. Asking students to simply memorize and then repeat spelling words doesn't ask them to understand those words, apply them in their own writing, break those words into their meaningful parts, use those parts to create a new and different word with a related meaning, or to evaluate their own writing or other's writing with the correct use of those words.

I know it's also easiest for parents to practice those spelling words with your kids because it feels like something simple to cross off the to-do list. Spelling words memorized? Check! But honestly, it's not the best use of your or your child's time. I need you to know that in many cases, there is not even an overall grade given for spelling alone. There often is not a separate spelling curriculum anymore, nor is there a box on the report card for a specific spelling grade.

Currently, teachers are encouraged to teach spelling in

applicable ways interwoven into reading and writing, not as an isolated subject. So it should not be the days of old with spelling workbooks and photocopied predictable worksheets to fill out or crossword puzzles to do. We're doing a serious disservice to our kids if we're making it all about spelling their lists correctly and getting that 100% or gold star at the top of the test.

That's not to say that spelling doesn't matter. We do need to be competent spellers, but nobody needs to be a perfect speller. Good spelling instruction should go beyond tricks and tips to memorize words, and aim for understanding. It's not a question of the old way versus the new way, but of teaching for complete understanding as opposed to mere memorization. Either way they'll do well on a test, but if they really understand words, they won't grow up wondering whether to use their, there, or they're when talking about their school experience.

What Happened to Cursive?

In addition to spelling, the teaching of cursive and emphasis on penmanship has changed dramatically in the last few decades. We say things like, "It's so sad. Kids don't even know how to write anymore," but the truth of the matter is we are waxing nostalgic about the good old days when things have simply changed.

I know I will have those who disagree, but handwriting just doesn't matter in the same way it used to. Precise penmanship in handwriting used to be the means of professional and personal communication. With the advent of the typewriter and now computers, tablets, and smart phones, the typed word is the most important and often preferred means of communicating personally and definitely professionally. We would never dream of handing in a handwritten resume, no matter how perfect our penmanship. So, we don't focus on teaching cursive because, frankly, it isn't important like it used to be to the futures of our students.

Now, does that mean we don't teach kids to write legibly using a pencil and paper? Absolutely not, but penmanship just isn't stressed anymore. My job is to prepare students for the actual future academic challenges and workplace they will enter, not teach them unnecessary skills for the sake of maintaining pretty handwriting.

The cheerleaders for the mandatory teaching of cursive in schools tend to cite the ability to write quickly and fluently as a main reason for still teaching it explicitly. This is a bit of a myth because the fact is: proper cursive is not a prerequisite to writing quickly or fluently.

Look at your own handwriting. It is most likely you use your own developed blend of cursive and printed letters. Kate Gladstone, an educator and handwriting expert herself, points out the invalidity of the fluency argument in an article for New York Times,

> "Adults increasingly abandon cursive. In 2012, handwriting teachers were surveyed at a conference hosted by Zaner-Bloser, a publisher of cursive textbooks. Only 37 percent

wrote in cursive; another 8 percent printed. The majority, 55 percent, wrote a hybrid: some elements resembling print-writing, others resembling cursive. When most handwriting teachers shun cursive, why mandate it?"(Gladstone 2013)[1]

Handwriting is an individualized thing. No two people's handwriting looks exactly alike even with the same training in forming letters. A first grade teacher can usually tell two children's handwriting apart after just a few weeks of school, because it is highly individual and will naturally differ.

Again, it's not that handwriting doesn't matter. We should absolutely be teaching kids to write legibly, and form letters properly, and to be able to distinguish between letters and write fluently. Students should be able to read back what they've written, and others should be able to read it as well. If we keep those goal in mind, we'll actually be doing our students a lot more good. It applies to many things— using invented spelling, writing legibly, etc. If a student writes a word, another can read it, and their thought was communicated, isn't that the point of writing and reading to begin with? In all reality, who cares if a child forms their a's with a tail or without a tail as long as you can tell it's an 'a'? Let's not let the means get in the way of the end.

Of course, all of this begs the question: Why can't we just teach it to preserve the tradition and beauty of cursive? Although many would acknowledge there isn't as big of a need to teach kids to write in cursive as there used to be, those same people nostalgically think it sad handwriting is going away. Based on my experience, I agree with Gladstone when she discusses what really matters when it comes to handwriting. She makes the case for teaching kids to read cursive, but not requiring them to necessarily write it.

> "Handwriting matters, but not cursive. The fastest, clearest handwriters join only some letters: making the easiest joins, skipping others, using print-like forms of letters whose cursive and printed forms disagree. Reading cursive matters, but even young children can be taught to read writing that they are not taught to produce. Reading cursive can be taught in just 30 to 60 minutes -- even to five or six-year-olds, once they read ordinary print. Why not teach children to read cursive, along with teaching other vital skills, including a handwriting style typical of effective handwriters?"(Gladstone 2013)[1]

What's the Harm?

Besides cursive not being as useful as it once was in terms of official communication, or as helpful as previously thought in terms of writing fluency, a lot of damage has actually been done in the past by demanding perfect penmanship. The harm is, for some kids, an overemphasis on handwriting and penmanship gets in the way of them actually writing.

After a child learns to write letters, you'll notice a totally normal preoccupation about how their writing looks. They have learned to form letters and are often frustrated that their fine motor development doesn't quite yet allow them to form them perfectly. For some kids this can be crippling in terms of their writing. It's very important in this stage to encourage process and legibility over perfection, and all too often, the emphasis is placed on the forming of letters at the expense of written expression.

Handwriting Without Tears is a handwriting program implemented in schools and occupational therapy programs across the country. The name should be an indication to you. If a program is titled Handwriting Without Tears, that implies that frequently handwriting is (or was) taught with tears. Writing is a complicated developmental process. It requires more mental and physical processes coordinating together than any other task we ask kids to do throughout a school day. From answering test questions to writing about what they've read, even lower level tasks like filling in worksheets require the act of writing. Think about that for a kid who struggles with the fine motor task of putting pencil to paper. If 30-60% of the school day requires kids to be writing, that can be excruciating for that child. Now add the demand of perfect, specific penmanship on top of that, and it seems impossible for an already struggling writer.

Keyboard vs Pencil

Technology is also playing an increasing role in writing

instruction. Kids now need to know typing and other technological skills that were not necessary decades ago. Although we don't focus as closely on handwriting in the classroom as we once did, the pendulum doesn't have to completely swing the other way. Doesn't this happen often in our culture? We throw the baby out with the bath water. It doesn't have to be technology vs. handwriting and proper spelling. Spell check does not make a good writer, any more than a calculator makes a good mathematician. The question should be how we can use all the tools in our arsenal to enhance the way we teach kids and give them better opportunities to communicate with the written word.

For example, as I'm writing this very chapter, I am going back and forth between a written outline in a notebook and the computer screen. I've found it helps me to scratch out some ideas the old-fashioned way, organizing them with pen and paper when I get stuck on a particular section in my manuscript. The goal should be to teach kids multiple writing strategies, how to use them, and when certain skills might be more helpful.

The positive impact of technology in meeting the needs of diverse learners in modern classrooms can also not be ignored. I've personally found it extremely effective in helping struggling writers express themselves. Tyler was a student of mine in my third grade class. Every morning, we began the day with writing in our journals, and every morning was a struggle with Tyler. He had some emotional and behavioral challenges, and writing in his journal seemed to set him off. He would cry about how hard it was some days and other days just flat out refuse to do anything. At worst he would have a complete emotional meltdown over writing in his journal, at best he would quietly refuse.

I gave it some time at the beginning of the school year, thinking maybe he just needed to get into the routine and consistency would help the situation, but it didn't improve. I hated starting every day with conflict, and knew it was setting Tyler up for a rough rest of the day. So, I decided to try an alternative option. I told Tyler he could write his journal entries on the computer instead of a notebook. He loved the computer, and I thought typing his journal might remove the fine motor difficulty of writing for him and help him to focus on his ideas. It worked! It was silly we had wasted so much time trying to force him to write in a notebook, when the same task could be accomplished on the computer.

Misunderstanding the New Ways

Many would argue that losing the old ways of teaching certain subjects encourages laziness, both mentally and otherwise. They imply concentration on nice penmanship and perfect spelling is really more about the discipline. While they may have a point about the discipline of "kids these days," If we're being honest, I think that has a lot more to do with changing societal and behavioral expectations (see Chapters 2 and 3), than it does spelling and cursive.

I think of it much like farming. For ages, all farm work was done by hand, or with very basic tools. It took much longer, required much more man power and was far less efficient. Now we have machinery which aids farmers and workers in preparing the soil, sowing seeds, and maintaining and harvesting crops. While there is value in a hard day's work in the dirt with your hands, we cannot ignore the changing landscape of farming and the need to keep up with the demands of the time in order to be productive and feed your family.

Like farming, there is definite value in preserving and learning about more traditional ways of doing things in the classroom. But innovation and efficiency are also important when deciding how to spend limited classroom time and resources.

So it's not that we don't teach things like proper handwriting or spelling, we just might teach them differently than in the past, and ideally in better ways. We've learned from the mistakes of the past, and are conscious of making choices in the best interest of learners. There is a finite amount of time in any given school day, and it is necessary to make choices, so at a certain point it boils down to educational efficiency. Spelling, handwriting, and other traditional conventions are still important, and they are still being taught. It's that we've found a time and a place to emphasize those things, and as I mentioned earlier, expecting perfection from the onset of any developmental task can discourage the task altogether.

For example, as I write this book, there is a process I follow. Checking for things like grammar, punctuation, and spelling is the very last step of the process. First, I brainstorm ideas, organize them, write a rough draft, revise that draft, have others review it, then comes the final edit where I make sure every 'i' is dotted and every 't' crossed. It would have been counterproductive for me to focus on things like spelling during the brainstorming or rough draft phase. I do need an understanding of words and their parts and how to manipulate them to get my point across, but I saved the polish of perfect spelling and grammar for the last step.

That's how writing is now taught to our kids. By allowing them to get their ideas down on paper first, and then treating their writing with an authentic process similar to that of the real world, we are providing a more beneficial example and encouraging young writers.

A common misconception when discussing the old way vs new way of teaching things like spelling, handwriting, and other writing conventions is that they just flat out aren't being taught anymore. In reality, they're simply being taught differently, and in the proper order, with the proper emphasis.

"Has teaching been done if learning has not occurred? If a child cannot apply a spelling pattern or writing convention accurately, it is our responsibility, as educators and parents, to come together to develop an alternate teaching plan to ensure academic growth and self-efficacy. When students believe they can achieve, they are on the road to academic excellence."

Aubrey Ruhser,
Assistant Principal/Literacy Specialist

CHAPTER NINE: *READING, WRITING, AND HOW TO RAISE KIDS WHO DO BOTH*

One of my favorite students of all time was Travis. I know, I know, teachers are not supposed to have favorites, but we do. There's a behind the scenes secret for you. When you are with kids all day for an entire school year, some just find a special place in your heart. Travis was one of those kids who soaked up life and learning like a sponge. He was a bright and clumsy student, with a perpetually messy desk and a quirky sense of humor. He asked lots of questions and invented stories. I called him my mad scientist. He was particularly interested in anything scientific fascinated by whales.

At one point in the school year, his life's mission became to read Moby Dick, right then, in third grade. Although a very strong reader, he was obviously not quite ready for Herman Melville's 635 page classic, so the librarian at our school tried to help him find a condensed children's version of the story. She hadn't succeeded until she spotted just such a version in the $2.00 bin at the grocery store. Before school started the next morning, she came rushing into my classroom to show me what she'd found. She knew Travis would be thrilled, and asked if I could send him down to the library at some point in the day so she could give it to him.

After the bell rang, and the students settled in as I took attendance, I called Travis up to my desk. "Hey Travis, Mrs. Nomack has something for you in the library. She wanted me to send you down there to pick it up." His brow furrowed with confusion, but he smirked and tripped over his feet as he jetted off to the library.

When he returned a few minutes later, he ran up to me with his child-friendly version of Moby Dick held out proudly. "Look what she found!" he grinned.

"That's awesome, Travis." I replied. "I know how much you've wanted to read that! I hope you made sure to thank Mrs. Nomack?"

"Wait," he said with wide eyes. "Did she . . . I mean . . . is this . . . is this mine to keep?" he asked hugging the book to his chest, practically blinking back tears.

"You know, I'm not sure about that one actually," I said. "I guess I don't know if she meant it to be for the library, or just for you to have. You better go ask her if you can keep it just to be sure." Out the door he ran again to ask her if the book was his to keep.

A few quick minutes later the classroom door swung open

wide, and he stood there with the book held high in the air. "Call me Ishmael!" he shouted. "She said yes!"

I immediately filed this story away in my mind under, Reasons Why I Teach. There is nothing like the magic of a child fully excited about reading. As a passionate reader and writer myself, I know the worlds that have opened to me from the pages of a great book. I know what it's like to read someone else's words and feel like they are telling your story, making the world a less lonely place. Writing is also a major part of who I am. It is like breathing for me to notice the world around me, and write about it. Putting my life and stories down on paper makes them matter and helps me see my life through a lens of purpose.

Beyond the enjoyment and connectedness that literacy brings to our lives, academically, reading and writing are the foundations for everything else. As they go through school, students are asked to do more with reading and writing than any other skills. That's why so much time is spent, especially in the early years of education, laying a foundation for literacy. Kids will use reading and writing in every other area of study. Math, science, and social studies all require reading, and then writing about what you've read or learned.

Literacy is also crucial to life skills beyond school. A well-read adult who can communicate effectively through the written word is a successful person, no matter what career path they choose later in life. Our job as parents and teachers then is to raise readers and writers and help them grow into literate adults, a trait that can't hurt no matter what their chosen path might be.

Raising Readers

My niece Norah practically came out of the womb with a book in her hand. She has had an insatiable appetite for books her whole young life. She is four years old now, and I have never seen a child her age with quite this kind of attention span for books.

Christmas morning, with shredded wrapping paper everywhere and new toys beckoning, we watched her sit on the floor in a pile of all her new books contentedly turning pages for over an hour at two years old. Before she could talk in complete sentences she would be retelling a story or making one up while turning a book's pages saying things like, "dat's a witch!" on one page, turning the page, then, "dat's a pwoblem."

When she was potty training, my brother told me how frustrated she would get about the interruption to her day when constantly having to go sit on the toilet and try to use the bathroom. She was very busy, often reading, and couldn't be bothered with being asked if she needed to go potty every half hour. I suggested to my brother to take all her favorite books, put them in a basket in the bathroom, and tell her she can read them while she sits on the potty.

Norah had a natural interest in books from very early on, but I believe it can be fostered in all children. Children are naturally curious, and sometimes we make reading more complicated than it needs to be. The first thing we can do to encourage the love of books, is follow the child's lead. While all books are not created equally, and there is a definite difference between quality children's literature and other children's books, I believe for the purposes of creating an interest in books early on, any book will do. If your son wants to read nothing but Thomas the Train books at first, then I say "choo choo." If your daughter incessantly brings you Dr. Seuss books to read until you start speaking in nothing but rhymes, just go with it. Read them in the house. Read them with a mouse. Read them in a box. Read them with a fox (Sorry, got carried away).

The point is, any book that your child is interested in, even if it's just for the pictures, is a good book for developing a love of reading. Nobody does anything they don't like to do. So the first step in creating avid readers is for children to like reading. Sometimes we skip that part, and even unintentionally do things that discourage early reading.

As I mentioned in Chapter 1, if you've been doing things like reading books, singing songs, and coloring with your child, you've already provided them with a great base for learning in school. But for those who want to know the next steps to raising readers, I'll let you in on some secrets. It's not that complicated. (Are you sensing a "keep it simple" theme to my philosophy about teaching children?)

Beyond enjoying books, the next step to reading and writing any language is actually using that language. Creating readers and writers is best done by first creating speakers and listeners. Use language often. Have conversations with your kids, and ask them questions. This might seem obvious, but I think we often get busy with the day or don't know how to talk to kids. We think we need to use baby talk or some special kind of kid speak, but simply talking to them about what you're doing naturally fosters language development.

Sing songs and recite rhymes together. "The Itsy Bitsy Spider" is more than just a cutesy song about a persistent little arachnid. It's full of rhyme, repetition, and patterns, which are important, because they develop a child's phonological awareness (a fancy way of saying that kids are aware and have an understanding of the sounds that make up words). This awareness is the first essential step to being able to use phonics (the understanding that sounds and printed letters are connected) to read and write words.

Besides building a strong language base with your child, filling your home with the written word is another simple way to encourage reading. Surround yourself and your child with words and books. In the teaching world, we call this creating a print-rich environment, and the beauty of it is that any print counts. Fill your home with kid books and adult books. Read recipes and articles. Notice print around you. Read street signs together. Ask your child what the word underneath the golden arches says when you stop at the drive-thru. They don't know why that says McDonald's, but they have learned that the word on that big sign stands for something, and it leads to chicken nuggets and a happy meal toy.

That's reading! Connecting words to meaning—it's a start.

Use print in less conventional ways too. Besides reading books, children can make words out of play dough, blocks, or Legos. Decorate their room with signs and use the letters in their name as a learning tool. New learning needs to be relevant to the learner. So when a child starts school, their name is one of the first things we use to teach letters, because nothing is more relevant and personal to a child at that age than their name.

"You're a Reader!"

Reading is a developmental process, and kids all learn to do it at different rates. It's a challenge for lots of kids, so one of the best things you can do for your child while they are learning to read is to encourage them. Be their biggest cheerleader, and their most captivated listener. It pushes them on to persist at something completely abstract and foreign to them at first, and it plays a huge role in shaping their attitudes about reading.

A phrase I use all the time to praise children for exhibiting early reading behaviors is "You're a reader!" I follow it up with pointing out a specific skill they used while reading. For example, "You're a reader! You used the pictures to help you tell the story. That's what good readers do." Or instead of immediately correcting a misread word, I might say "I like how you went back and fixed that word when it didn't make sense. Readers think and make sure what they're reading makes sense to them."

I've seen so many adults unintentionally discourage kids, because a child might be reading from memorization of a familiar book or retelling the story based on the pictures. Please don't say things to your child like, "You're not really reading that yet. You just memorized it." Retelling a story from memory is a part of reading, and it's definitely a prerequisite to true independent reading. When they retell their own version of a familiar story, they are practicing valuable comprehension skills like remembering what happened at the beginning, middle, and end of a story. They are recalling important events and explaining what the characters did and said. They're summarizing the story showing you they understand what was read to them. Reading from left to right, turning pages, and understanding that text on a page has meaning connected to the pictures on that page are all important concepts of print that they will need as readers. Those things are crucial parts of reading, and they're practicing them while they retell a story to you from memory, turning pages as they go. If those habits are discouraged as "not really reading" kids can be discouraged early on.

Sometimes adults are surprised and even disagree when teachers and other professionals tell them to let kids make mistakes while reading. They wonder: Why would we let them keep doing things the wrong way? Aren't we just reinforcing bad habits, then?

It's actually much like learning to walk. You don't discourage a kid every time they fall down and wobble while learning to walk because you know those first wobbly, tentative steps are the beginnings of something greater. You don't say, "Nope! Try again. That's not walking, it's wobbling." You excitedly praise them even when it looks more like drunken lurching and falling down. You proudly show it off to everyone while they hold on to your one finger because you know that walking is a developmental process. Children learn to roll over, crawl, pull themselves up to standing, and wobble before they walk and eventually run. It doesn't mean those first few steps aren't walking, just because they are not fluid or perfect.

Finally, any teacher will tell you, the most important, worthwhile thing you can do as a parent to raise a future reader is to read aloud with your child. Mem Fox is an acclaimed children's book author of several great stories like, Hattie and the Fox, Ten Little Fingers and Ten Little Toes, and Wilfrid Gordon McDonald Partridge. On her website, she lays out her Ten Read-Aloud Commandments, which I think are the key to reading aloud with your children:

> "Spend at least ten wildly happy minutes every single day reading aloud. From birth!

> Read at least three stories a day: it may be the same story three times. Children need to hear a thousand stories before they can begin to learn to read. Or the same story a thousand times!

Read aloud with animation. Listen to your own voice and don't be dull, or flat, or boring. Hang loose and be loud, have fun and laugh a lot.

Read with joy and enjoyment: real enjoyment for yourself and great joy for the listeners

Read the stories that your child loves, over and over, and over again, and always read in the same 'tune' for each book: i.e. with the same intonations and volume and speed, on each page, each time.

Let children hear lots of language by talking to them constantly about the pictures, or anything else connected to the book; or sing any old song that you can remember; or say nursery rhymes in a bouncy way; or be noisy together doing clapping games.

Look for rhyme, rhythm, or repetition in books for young children, and make sure the books are really short.
Play games with the things that you and the child can see on the page, such as letting kids finish rhymes, and finding the letters that start the child's name and yours, remembering that it's never work, it's always a fabulous game.

Never ever teach reading, or get tense around books.

Please read aloud every day because you just adore being with your child, not because it's the right thing to do"(Fox 2013).[1]

Early Writing

Just like reading, writing can and should be encouraged in all kinds of ways from very early on. Reading and writing are naturally and inextricably linked. You cannot be a good reader, without learning to write, and it's impossible to be a good writer who cannot read.

Therefore, much like raising readers, raising writers can occur in natural ways connected to reading, throughout the day with your child. Even though reading might seem to be a bit easier to integrate into daily life, writing first starts with something as simple as coloring with crayons, as I talked about in Chapter 1. Making scribbles on a page with a crayon is really one of the first steps to writing. While coloring, children are learning to hold a writing utensil. They're learning the cause and effect of writing, that if they move their hands in a certain way, it creates a corresponding image on the paper. They're also learning the control and fine motor skills necessary to write.

The next thing you'll notice your little one doing is mimicking writing they see you do. They might write a note or list. They might use a notepad and pretend to take everyone's order at a restaurant while scribbling across the page quickly like they've seen adults do. Ask them to help you make a grocery list by writing down what you need, even copying your words after you write them. Drawing pictures and scribbling to communicate on paper is the next step before writing words.

They start making letter like shapes, circles and lines. All letters in the English alphabet are formed from certain combinations of circles and straight, slanted, or curved lines. Letters are the foundation of words, and words are the foundation of sentences and sharing thoughts on paper. After they are making letter shapes, next move on to writing a child's name. Learning needs to be relevant, so using their name has meaning to them immediately.

Once they know how to make letters and words, they will begin labeling things they draw. They might draw a picture of all the members of their family, with each person's name written near that person in the picture. This is huge! They are learning that a group of letters put together form a word, and that word stands for something.

"You're a Writer!"

When kids are in these early stages, much like with reading, the most important thing you can do is to encourage them. I see parents get a little panicky at first when their child is spelling the word "cake" like "kak." There's a dilemma about what to do when your child asks, "Is that how you spell cake?" If your child is still in the stage of first learning that letters make certain sounds in words, and that those letters are strung together to make words, then yes, they spelled cake. Now, I also believe in being honest with kids. So, I wouldn't say, "Yup that's exactly how you spell cake." I would say something like, "I see your picture of the birthday cake, and I see you heard those sounds in that word and wrote them there. I hear all those sounds in that word too. I can read that word, cake. You are a writer! Good writers try new words by writing down the sounds they hear."

Letting go of the perfect way to spell it may make you a little itchy at first, but don't worry. Just because you encourage the good things your child is doing when writing that word, does not mean they will go through life thinking "cake" is spelled "kak." Eventually your little one will learn the rule for silent e at the end of words, but in the meantime they are focusing on forming their thoughts into writing. We don't ever want to discourage that. When we value the process over perfection, we teach kids to take risks in their writing. We teach them it's more important to write and create and put their thoughts to paper, than to spell every one of those thoughts perfectly.

Growing Readers

Eventually (and usually around third grade), learning to read becomes reading to learn. They go from simply learning how to read, to being expected to use those reading skills to use and learn about something else. They go from learning to read words like "civil" knowing that the c makes an /s/ sound in some words when followed by an i or e, to reading about the Civil War and being asked about the causes of the war.

Often when kids are independent readers, we forget their reading skills are still developing. They are using reading in new ways and need to work on skills like content-based literacy, or critical analysis of texts. I would argue we don't spend enough time on these skills as kids get older. Often we think we've taught them to read, so they're good to go for the rest of their lives, but all reading is not the same. We read nonfiction books differently than we read novels. Magazine and newspaper articles are read and understood differently than comic books or graphic novels. It's also not just an English/Language Art's teacher's job to teach literacy. All teachers have a responsibility to make sure students have the understanding to use the specific kinds of reading skills necessary to access various types of content.

Just because children are using reading in more sophisticated ways, also doesn't mean they can't still enjoy it. In fact, as reading demands increase at school, reading for enjoyment at home becomes even more important. Sometimes we forget to make reading fun for older kids, or encourage it as purposefully as we do when they're younger. Give books as gifts based on your child's interests. Older children tend to love reading books in series. Help them find a series to get into. Don't stop reading aloud when they reach a certain age. Everyone loves to be read to, and a great rule of thumb is just to choose a book slightly above their independent reading level to read together. You could even consider special reading privileges, like allowing them to stay up later as long as they're reading a book. Continue to be intentional about making reading a priority, even with your older children.

Encouraging Writing with Older Children

Likewise, learning to write becomes writing about what you've learned as children get older. Kids start to write book reports and research papers as early as second grade. They are asked to formulate their own thoughts about a specific topic, and then communicate those thoughts through writing. This is a major step up in difficulty from just learning how to write words and then sentences, to stringing those sentences together to prove what they know about something.

Writing is the highest form of using language. It requires more coordinated effort than almost any other academic task, and is required of students more often than any other task besides reading. When writing a response to a test question for example, children will need to combine the physical process of writing with what they know about grammar and sentence structure, putting their thoughts in an order that makes sense with some style and sophistication. Sometimes they are even under a time limit to do so. We are asking a lot from students as they get older, and that's why a solid foundation of writing skills is so important. If some of those things, like the physical act of writing, the rules of grammar, and using language are more automatic, the writing becomes less difficult and students can focus on their ideas and how best to convey them.

When your children have moved past the stage of making letters out of play dough or pretending to take your order at their imaginary restaurant, how can you encourage writing at home? There are lots of ideas for creating inspiration and writing opportunities with your older kiddos. You could give them a journal or diary. As kids get older they love to record secrets and feelings and privacy becomes very important, so they tend to love their very own place to pour out their thoughts on the page. You could also start an interactive journal with your child, in which you write notes back and forth to each other in the same notebook. Sometimes even a moody tween or teen who doesn't want to talk has an easier time communicating in writing. So it's a great way to encourage writing and communication at the same time.

Use technology to your advantage, and email or text back and forth with your kids. You might be amazed at how much you will communicate with your child if you're willing to do so via text. Besides using writing as a valuable communication tool, encourage creative writing with your kids. Allow them to create gifts for family members and friends using writing-like a poem or card about how special they are to them. Publish their stories. Children and adults of all ages love to have their work published. Teach them how to use a word processing program or look into applications that turn older children's more sophisticated ideas into books.

Above all, take a genuine interest in your child's writing. Encourage them to share it with you and others. Respond thoughtfully, but not critically to what they have written. Allow for some writing to remain private, in journals or diaries, but make room for some writing to be shared and celebrated.

As you can see, there are some real simple things you can do on a daily basis with your kids of all ages to encourage literacy. Reading and writing are important skills essential to your child's future success no matter what, but that's not the only reason to support children's development in those areas. Not only does your support create readers and writers, but it gives you meaningful opportunities to connect with your child.

Don't miss out on the magic of hearing your child read you a book for the very first time all by themselves. Enjoy that first apology note you find slid under your bedroom door after an argument. Reading and writing opens up whole new worlds to your child and your relationship with them. I wouldn't want you to miss a second of it just because you're overthinking it or worried you're not doing it right.

"Reading is the gateway to learning. It opens up understanding and links you to places and experiences you might have never had. It is the basis for all learning, and once you create a student who loves reading, the possibilities of learning in all aspects of school become richer."

Stacey Noel, Media Specialist

"Building a strong literacy foundation is one of the greatest things a parent can do for a child. It is not 'rocket science' and parents should not be intimated by it. It can be achieved by simply spending quality time with your child while exposing them to new things, asking them thoughtful questions, reading to and with them, and simply engaging in a conversation with them. It really is that simple!"

Vicki Foley, First Grade Teacher

CHAPTER TEN: *CARDS, DICE, AND WHY EVERYONE CAN DO MATH*

"Hi, what's your birthday?" Molly would ask every child and adult she came in contact with, barely able to contain her excitement. Molly had autism, and also a unique gift for being able to tell you, on-the-spot, the exact day of the week your birthday would fall on during that calendar year. When a friend told her what his or her birthday was, she would look up, deep in concentration for only a few seconds, and then excitedly declare, "Your birthday's on a Thursday!" or "Your birthday's Saturday this year!"

The first few times she did it, the classroom assistant who worked with Molly looked it up on a calendar to see if her prediction was accurate. It always was, and after a while no one questioned it. She pulled out this fun little game time after time, and was so pleased at her friend's amusement when she could tell them what day their birthday would be.

In second grade, we learned a lot about time and calendars, so Molly's special talent became a centerpiece of our lessons. "Molly's so good at this!" kids would notice. They started asking her for help with their work, and enjoyed playing math games with her.

One of the goals Molly had been working on was to initiate appropriate social interactions with peers. She struggled with social skills, but was great at math, so math started to become a means for her to connect. I was just as impressed by her quick calculation skills and ability to recognize patterns as I was with her ability to use math, a subject that many people despise, to overcome a social barrier and find a way to connect with her friends.

Molly's birthday math skill was more than just a parlor trick. It was an icebreaker to a bigger conversation. After she told other students what day of the week their birthday would be, they would then ask her, "When's your birthday, Molly?" and it would start a conversation about what day of the week her birthday fell on, and would eventually lead to what she wanted for her birthday. She and a friend would talk about where their birthday party was going to be, and their favorite flavors of cake. She was using the universal language of math to connect over something that was relevant to everyone—their birthdays.

Math is a common struggle for many students and adults, but it was not Molly's particular struggle. In fact, math actually helped her overcome some of her other challenges with social interactions. It worked because Molly was using math in a relevant, interesting way. I know many of us struggled with math as a subject in school, but I think if it was presented in more relevant, interesting ways, the results might have been different. Even as adults, we might be haunted by awful memories of long division or algebra. We may get sweaty palms when we have to figure out how much to leave for a tip. I can't count the number of times a parent of one of my students has told me, "Yeah, I'm awful at math. She gets that from me," or "I just don't have the math gene, so I won't be the one helping him with his homework."

As the adults with the most influence on your children, I want you to know your attitude about math (or anything for that matter) will shape your child's attitude about it. I want to help you to see math is not something we either have the gene for, or don't. While we definitely all have certain strengths and weaknesses, I want to blow the myth out of the water that you or your child "can't do math."

If you ask me, the reason math is such a common struggle is because of the way it's been taught (and sometimes still is being taught to our kids). We were taught math the wrong way in many cases, and our own attitudes as teachers and parents are sometimes getting in the way of our children's success. Here's the truth: There's no such thing as someone who can't do math. I'd like to help bring math back to life with some practical ideas.

No Such Thing as a Math Gene

Much like anything else, kids' attitudes and confidence around their math abilities start at home. The idea that one either gets math for life, or does not, is common in a lot of homes. In my classroom, I noticed that kids were most often successful in math when they didn't realize they were doing math. They had to be tricked into using everyday life situations to understand mathematical concepts. Seeing this made me think about how often adults probably don't realize they are "doing math." Each time you go shopping you are doing math. When you load up your cart, compare two items, decide if you can afford everything, or decide if something is worth it to you, that's math. Every time you use your calendar or a clock to figure out how much sleep you will get if your child actually stays in bed from now until morning? Math. Every time you try to decide if you have enough diapers to last until you go to the store tomorrow? Each time you measure for a recipe? That's math.

You do many of these things without much effort, and yet math is perceived to be harder for people than it actually is. It's a cultural monologue we keep reciting out loud. "Math is boring. Math is hard. I'm no good at it." Is it any wonder we begin to believe these things?

In my classroom, I did not see a major difference in a child's inherent ability to do math. What I saw was a major difference in their attitudes about math. That's not to say kids didn't have varying strengths and weaknesses across the curriculum, but I see something happening in math more than anywhere else in the curriculum—we make excuses.

Blaming something on genetics means it's beyond our control. It means that no matter what we do, some kids will learn it and some kids won't. It would mean then, for those kids who "don't get math," nothing we do makes a difference. That's simply not true. Unfortunately the idea that you either "get math" or you don't, is often perpetuated and made even worse in schools. John Mighton, founder of Jump Math, a nonprofit whose math curriculum is used in classrooms serving 65,000 children in grades one through eight and by 20,000 children at home, points out the problem in an article by David Bornstein for the New York Times.

> "Almost every kid — and I mean virtually every kid — can learn math at a very high level, to the point where they could do university level math courses. If you ask why that's not happening, it's because very early in school many kids get the idea that they're not in the smart group, especially in math. We kind of force a choice on them: to decide that either they're dumb or math is dumb. Children come into school with differences in background knowledge, confidence, ability to stay on task and, in the case of math, quickness. In school, those advantages can get multiplied rather than evened out"(Bornstein 2011).[1]

Unfortunately we are often reinforcing the idea that students either get math or they don't based on the attitudes about math teachers convey in the classroom. I have to be honest when I say, in addition to negative attitudes about math developed at home, I don't think we're doing a great job of teaching math in our schools, and I think that has a greater impact than genetics.

When Will I Ever Use This?

Math is all around us. Almost everything we do in a day involves mathematics to some degree. But, when it comes to teaching math in schools, we've isolated it and shoved it into text books, reducing it to formulas, and taking it out of its place in the real world for our students. Many of us were taught math that way ourselves.

I would venture to say you were probably taught math similarly to how I was—on a chalkboard, with the teacher or another student figuring out a complicated formula while perhaps you daydreamed or passed notes. Then you were assigned some problems out of the math book to do yourself, mostly at home, that were turned in for a grade.

You probably had a review session before a test where the teacher went over the kinds of problems you might see on the exam, and then you took a test and it was a big part of your grade. Unless you had a particularly passionate math teacher, math may have seemed boring and static and begged the question, "When am I ever going to use this?"

Math is very concrete, so you can teach it many ways, but getting to the right answer does matter. Therefore it's often taught the easy way, the way that requires the least amount of effort and (unfortunately), thought on the part of the teacher. Kids are taught formulas and memorize procedures to produce the right answer.

I, myself, found a particular kind of satisfaction in long

division, plugging in numbers and chugging away at formulas. There was something neat and concrete about it, but that was about it. I was learning a specific list of steps and how to perform them to get an answer. But I wasn't learning anything about why those steps worked, or applying what I was learning to the world around me.

I've always had a great memory, paid attention in class, and generally worked pretty quickly. So early on, I was deemed "good at math" and placed in advanced math classes. Being in the advanced classes made me feel like I was capable of doing math, and so I did. All through middle school and high school I was in the accelerated classes, which eventually led me to calculus and Mr. Ertle my senior year.

On the surface, Mr. Ertle seemed to be the stereotypical calculus teacher. He was shy and quiet, and clumsily shuffled into the classroom every day with a pocket protector and a stack of papers. I went to high school right in the middle of the inner city, with all the typical problems associated with such schools, so Mr. Ertle did not exactly fit in. He wasn't concerned about being cool or gimmicky. He was concerned that we knew he cared deeply about us and the subject he was teaching.

His eyes would light up and he would become animated, literally bouncing and hopping when explaining the way math made the world work. He knew math had to leap off the chalkboard, out of the text books, and walk around among us for us to learn it. He made a game for us with buzzers made out of film canisters hooked up to a computer. We would work in groups on a problem together and could buzz in with the answer, Family Feud style. We then had to explain how we got to the answer to get the team points. When he was absent, he videotaped lessons from home. His dedication was one thing, but his passion for showing us how this abstract, scary world of calculus could be real and relevant for us was what really stands out to me.

It is unfortunate that I had to wait until my last year of high school to get such an exemplary math teacher, and even more unfortunate that I only got to experience his teaching because I was on the "good at math" track. Mr. Ertle had it right when it came to teaching math, but he was the exception instead of the rule. He knew his own enthusiasm and dedication, high expectations, and tons of guidance and support would turn us into students who could actually do calculus. He was truly a passionate master of the subject matter he was teaching. How can a teacher pass on a love for a subject, and a deep understanding of it, without first loving it and deeply understanding it themselves? He also had high expectations both for himself and us. He was dedicated beyond the call of duty, probably, and his dedication set the bar high for us, motivating us to do better. He understood that learning takes place in small steps, with lots of support, and over time.

Current math curriculum and teaching methods still tend to teach too many concepts in isolation, without making connections for our students to prior learning. When kids are struggling with a particular concept, like multiplication for example, we say things like, "Multiplication is hard. They are just not getting it," instead of thinking about the prerequisite skills to being able to multiply they might be missing.

On top of that, with increased pressure to cover material, especially in math, we don't take the time to go back and fill gaps in learning or break things down into their smaller steps. We push on and leave many kids in the dust, without the fundamentals or confidence necessary. In the above mentioned article, David Bornstein gives an illustration of this:

> "Mighton found that to be effective he often had to break things down into minute steps and assess each student's understanding at each micro-level before moving on. Take the example of positive and negative integers, which confuse many kids. Given a seemingly straightforward question like, 'What is -7 + 5?' many will end up guessing. One way to break it down, explains Mighton, would be to say: 'Imagine you're playing a game for money and you lost seven dollars and gained five. Don't give me a number. Just tell me: Is that a good day or a bad day?'"(Bornstein 2011)[1]

What If We Taught Math More Like Reading?

Something dawned on me recently: we would never teach reading the way we still teach math. In reading instruction, educators spend a lot of time together discussing the merits of individual or small group time with the teacher each day, many repetitions of material, and careful analysis of gaps in student learning. We encourage lots of support and practice from home, and make sure they understand the foundational concepts before building upon them. We've been doing this in reading instruction for a long time, and it would be unheard of to talk about some kids "getting reading" and some not. We expect all kids to be able to read eventually, and we teach like it.

Teachers also spend a lot of time working on kids' feelings and attitudes toward reading. We read fun books, and encourage them to find their favorites. We build upon the skills they already have, and read as much as possible throughout the day. Teachers fill their classrooms with books, even creating cozy spaces for students to read, making it more appealing. We know nobody will read who doesn't like to. We do a much better job of acknowledging the power of attitude and motivation with reading than we do with math.

When a child is struggling in reading, we assume we need to back it up and slow down. We assume there are some gaps in learning that need to be filled, and that more practice is necessary. There is a lot of diagnostic investigation that goes into determining what the problem is when a child is having difficulty learning to read. Unfortunately with math, we don't usually do these same types of things. We isolate each individual skill too much and don't take advantage of the fact that it is easy to build upon small successes and expand on them in math.

For example, like we talked about earlier, if a child is having a hard time with multiplication, think of all the skills we could back up and make sure he's mastered before moving on to the next thing. Multiplication is combining equal groups or repeated addition. If students are struggling, you could back up to addition and make sure they are solid on that, or the concept of equal or groups. Math lends itself to building on small concepts and gradually increasing difficulty. Students experience success at each increasingly difficult level, and it instills confidence in them.

As a parent, you would never say, "I'm illiterate. She gets that from me." No parent has ever said to me, "Anything past third grade reading, and I'm of no use to help with homework." It's not socially acceptable to admit to being bad at reading, but it's almost seen as funny or a badge of honor to be bad at math. In fact, culturally speaking, people are even made fun of for being 'math geeks,' and it's not cool to be too good at or interested in math. Even if parents can't always make the time for it, most would acknowledge how important it is to read with their child every day. They know that their kid will only get better at reading with lots of practice and support. When a child is learning to read, we sit next to them, holding their hand through the process, giving them hints along the way, and building upon what they already know about letters, sounds, and words to gain meaning from the book. Parents should do those same things to support their child with math.

I think if we taught math with more enthusiasm and a better attitude, our kids would grow in confidence. If we taught like we expected all of our kids to get math with the proper support and practice, I think they would. If teachers and parents stopped treating math like a mystery that you either get or you don't, our kids would experience more success.

Bringing Math Back to Life

In the classroom, I often used cards and dice to teach math. This made math "fun," because students didn't realize they were doing math. I thought about how funny that was, the fact that we need to trick kids into doing math. What if it wasn't about tricking kids into doing math but pointing out the ways math really is fun and relevant? Breaking it down into smaller pieces so that students can feel successful and build on that success to gain confidence is also key. We all know that if you don't feel like you can do something, you won't.

So, here are some ways you can encourage positive attitudes about math in your home and create mathematicians that can and will do math:

Speak positively about math. If you want a child to be a strong reader, you would never go around the house saying, "I hate reading. Books are hard and confusing." Refraining from talking about math in negative ways is important too.

Play games. Games involving cards, dice, or dominoes are especially great for math skills, but almost any game can be great for math development. Skills like counting, logic, reasoning, and problem solving are all crucial math skills that are used when playing games.

Model math. For example, when you're at the grocery store with your kids, calculate your total out loud so you are modeling the use of math in relevant ways. Compare the amount of cereal in two different sized boxes. Ask kids questions about how many juice boxes you'll need for all the kids to have one every day in their lunch, or put them to work counting out ten oranges and putting them in the cart for you.

Let them help in the kitchen. Ask them to set the table for dinner. Making sure each person has a plate, a fork, and a glass teaches making sets and one-to-one correspondence. Cooking and baking together is also great for math development. When kids are little they are becoming familiar with measurement, and as they get older you can have them do the measuring or doubling of a recipe themselves.

Use money. You could give them a small allowance, and watch how naturally they are interested in math when saving to buy that new toy. Even something as simple as allowing them to pay the cashier at the store, or pulling out the change in your pocket and counting it together are easy ways to use math at home.

Sort it out. Sorting is a very important early math skill. Allow them to sort the laundry by color, or pair up socks. Putting silverware away from the dishwasher is another practical way to sort. It's so fun for kids to sort their toys or books on their own too. Talk about why they chose to put certain ones together.

Use the whining. When your kids are fighting over who gets the bigger half, use it as a chance for a mini lesson on what the fraction ½ really means. Show them how there's no such thing as a bigger half.

Time it. Using a timer to see how fast a child can get their room clean makes it a fun challenge and helps them become familiar with the concept of time. Talk about what time you are doing things, and point out the clock when it's time for a routine activity like, "Oh look. It's 12:00. Time for lunch," or "You can come out of your room on Saturday only after the clock says 7:00."

Learn about it together. When older children bring home math homework that seems hard or unfamiliar to you, instead of telling them you don't know how to do it that way, or complaining because it was not the way you were taught how to do it, say something like, "I've never seen how to do it that way. Can you show me how?" Even simply saying, "Let's figure this out together," positively communicates to your child you are there to help them and you don't have to have all the answers. It's a fun way to figure it out together.

Ask questions. Ask your kids questions about how they got their answer when working on a math problem. Ask them to explain what they did. Ask questions of your child's teacher if you don't understand why something is being taught a certain way. It might be different than the way you learned it, but there is more than one way to get the right answer.

Math instruction is one of those areas which continually changes. Many of us ended up hating math, so a change couldn't hurt right? There are concrete right and wrong answers, but the more we learn about how the brain works and how children develop, the more our methods need to change to meet that. Your child can do math, and so can you.

"In my own experience, if you can keep a kid confident in their skills, and they actually know what is going on in their homework, they not only do the work but take pride in it. It is not often that they don't do the work because they just don't want to. Kids get a sense of satisfaction when they perform a problem correctly, whether they admit it or not. The main goal of the teacher and parents should be instilling and maintaining that confidence."

Brian Buston, High School Calculus Teacher

CHAPTER ELEVEN: *REPORT CARDS, TESTING, AND WHAT REALLY MATTERS*

One of my third grade students, Derrick, was earning D's and F's first quarter in every subject due to missing or incomplete assignments. I had chatted with him many times about the fact that his parents would soon see his progress report, and suggested he might want to start doing his work. He seemed fairly un-phased, and had obviously not yet made the connection between work turned in and grades earned.

Not long after progress reports were sent home, I heard from Derrick's mom, and she understandably wanted to set up a meeting to discuss his grades. When I met with her the next morning she told me a funny, but telling, story.

"So first of all," she began, "I want you to know we talked with Derrick extensively about this progress report last night." She smirked as she told me the next part. "He came happily trotting through the door yesterday afternoon and handed me his progress report without a care in the world. I looked at it and was like, 'Derrick!' There are D's and F's all over this! What have you been doing?!?' He looked at me with genuine surprise at my reaction and in all seriousness said, 'Mom. It's not that bad. I mean I know it's not straight A's but it's not like there's Z's on it or anything.'"

She assured me she then explained to him the grading system did not go all the way to Z, and we both laughed at his innocent misunderstanding of how it all worked. We continued to make a plan to help him get organized, and get his work turned in complete and on time, but I was humbled and sheepish to realize I hadn't done a great job of explaining the grading scale. I had just assumed students knew what D's and F's meant for the most part. The very next day we had a class meeting explaining the point of grades and the correlation between work turned in and the grades on the progress report.

In a time when more emphasis than ever is placed on grades and test scores, Derrick's reaction clearly demonstrates how arbitrary those things can be to actual learning, and how oblivious children are to what they mean. Teachers and parents tend to get a little worked up about grades and test results. Parents may want the straight A student, and to proudly sport honor roll bumper stickers. Many teachers want the best test scores and a class full of conscientious little geniuses. And while there is nothing wrong with high expectations, in my opinion, this area of student evaluation has begun to get out of balance. The focus has shifted too far from measuring actual student learning to become about competition and pressure.

In addition to heavy emphasis placed on grades and achievement, the increased political and administrative pressure for higher test scores and more testing is intense. Added accountability is good, but we may need to reexamine our perspective on some of these things. I want to explore the areas of grading and testing further, discuss the role grades and tests should play in evaluating students, and give you some suggestions for how to keep those things in perspective. I want to help you encourage your children to do their best in an age where increasing importance is placed on student achievement.

Making the Grade

The story of Derrick was a common one when I taught third grade, because this was the first year my students received traditional letter grades on progress reports and report cards. Up to that point, from kindergarten through second grade, they had received numbers to indicate their performance toward meeting a particular standard or benchmark. For example, a 4 on the progress report indicated they were above the benchmark and exceeding current grade level expectations, while a 1 would indicate they were below grade level and needed more time and/or support. These were the kinds of "grades" students and parents were used to seeing, and it was a big switch to start earning the traditional A's, B's, and C's instead.

Many schools operate on a similar system, with students being evaluated quarterly with report cards and sometimes mid-quarterly with progress reports. Mid-quarter progress reports are intended to give parents a general idea of how their child is doing, and what grades they are earning up to that point.

I understand at the heart of some of the intensity around student grades is the basic question, "How am I doing?" As human beings, it is natural to want feedback on our work, to be reassured we're doing a good job. Kids want to know how they're doing. Parents want to know how their child is doing and what they can do to help them succeed. Almost every parent/teacher conference I've ever had started with the question, "How is he/she doing?" and I could read it between the lines of almost every parent email and concerned phone call.

It's understandable. Parents just want to know if their child is learning, keeping up, and staying on track. They want to know their child is ok, that he or she is not struggling too much, or bored and unchallenged. They rely on grades as a measure of those things. While good grades are important to academic achievement, it is important to keep them in perspective and remember that they are really only a summary of a bigger story.

So how do we keep grades in perspective? What is their proper role? How can you as a parent get an accurate picture of how your child is actually performing in the classroom? I think report cards and grades should be used as a summary. Think of it as a condensed overview of a student's progress, which gives a general picture of their performance in school. It should really summarize all of the ongoing communication among students, parents, and teachers about learning and areas of strength and weakness. If there was daily or weekly communication about how a child is doing, what they are struggling with, what their strengths are, and how parents and teachers can best support the child's learning, grades would never come as a surprise or be taken too seriously. There would be an understanding of what went into the child earning that grade, and an understanding of any modifications or accommodations necessary to grade them on the same scale as everyone else.

Students earn grades, teachers don't arbitrarily give them. But, teachers have the responsibility to communicate how those grades are being earned, and any concerns they may have. When parents were upset over grades, it usually came down to my lack of communication with them about what went into that grade, or the fact that a student was struggling long before report cards came home. I've learned that a grade should never be a surprise to any student or parent, because the parent should already be aware of any struggles, and participating in a plan to help the student improve. If I have done my job as a teacher in evaluating that student and communicating effectively about their progress, a grade (good or bad) should reflect that ongoing conversation.

Most importantly, keep in mind each school, grade level, and teacher grades differently. Those grading systems also vary according to state, district, and individual school policies and expectations. So staying informed as the parent will also be very important. To help make sense of how your child will be graded, here are some things you can do to be proactive:

Review the school/district grading policy. Be sure you are familiar with how often your child will be graded, how those grades will be communicated to you, and what each grade means.

Review the individual teacher's grading policy or syllabus. Be sure to go over this with your child as well. You both should be familiar with how different areas weigh in to the overall grade. Be sure you both have an understanding of how homework, class work, test, and project grades are combined to earn an overall grade.

For projects graded subjectively, ask to see a scoring rubric. A rubric is a commonly used tool, which is a guide listing specific criteria for grading those projects. Teachers use it to ensure students know what is expected of them for the project and how they will be evaluated. It also helps to ensure consistency in grading when applied uniformly.

Be an advocate for your child. If something doesn't seem to be adding up, set up a time to talk to the teacher about it. Ask questions. Perhaps there is a mistake in calculating the grade, or the grading policy needs to be revisited. If approached respectfully, most teachers appreciate your thoughtful feedback and want to make sure their grading systems reflect student learning as accurately as possible.

Not All Data is Good Data

Beyond grades, a huge emphasis is also placed on data in our schools, most of which is derived from scores on classroom, district, and state tests. We collect data on every student, compile it in binders, and have meetings to discuss data. This can be a great thing. We should absolutely be using data to drive our instruction and make informed decisions about the best ways to teach our kids. As a teacher, I have welcomed data in its meaningful forms. Data backs up a teacher's, or parent's, hunches. It shows growth, and quantifies some of those more intangible aspects of learning. We can see exactly where some holes are in student learning, areas of concern, and red flags. Data is not a bad thing, but when certain standardized test scores are the primary or only thing looked at in terms of data, or when data is collected and analyzed incorrectly, it becomes a major problem. Just as with grading, a balance is necessary when we talk about testing and evaluating students, teachers, and schools based on the data from those tests.

In education right now, we're a bit out of balance. As a parent, you may be overwhelmed with test results and data reports on your student at every parent/teacher conference. It may seem your child is taking some important test every week. The language and acronyms alone are enough to drive everyone batty. Oh you don't know what NCLB, CCSS, DIBELS, AIMS, DRA, and WKCE are? Don't worry. We have trouble keeping them all straight too.

It's time for some full testing disclosure. . . teachers are just as confused and frustrated by some of it as you are. Every single year I have taught, some new standardized test or diagnostic tool has crossed my path to collect data on my students. And by crossed my path, I mean forced onto me and my students with maybe an hour of after school training on how to administer it. Then teachers are put in the unfortunate position of explaining the verbiage, reason for, and merits of these tests to you as parents. We also need to motivate our students to take it and do their best on it, because in one way or another, their results on some of these tests will likely be tied to our performance evaluations and perhaps even our pay. So I'd like to cut through some of the lingo and politics of testing, and help make some sense of the different types of tests your kids might be taking, being honest about the merits and limitations of each.

Teaching to the Test

You may not realize it, but the main point of most classroom assessments—from informal quizzes to end of unit tests—is actually to determine how we are doing as teachers. Formative assessments are the type most commonly used in the classroom for the purposes of informing our instruction as teachers. Formative assessment includes a series of formal and informal checks to tell us what students know, what they don't know, and whether we need to reteach something or move on. They are methods we use to monitor the learning process as it happens. Classroom assessments are not high stakes and some are not even connected to grades. They provide an informal way for us to adjust our teaching in real time to meet the needs of all our learners.

For example, before teaching a science unit on water, I might ask my students to first brainstorm and write down everything they know about water. This is a very informal pre-test which tells me what knowledge the students already bring to the table on the topic, as well as any misconceptions I may need to address.

After teaching on water for a while, I might then give a quick one question quiz, asking students to name the three main states of the water (solid, liquid, gas). If most/all of my students answer the question correctly, I know we can move on to other topics like the water cycle, or water as a resource. If it's clear most of my students do not know the three states, I would spend some time re-teaching and clarifying before moving on to make sure the whole class has a basic understanding.

Finally, I might give an end of unit test on all the material covered in relation to water. Ideally they will do relatively well, because I have been informally assessing their progress throughout the unit, and adjusting my teaching accordingly. However if every student bombs the test, it indicates a problem with my teaching or even the test itself. We want to know how our students are doing, and as an extension, how we are doing as teachers.

Many school districts also administer some type of test district-wide. In addition to assessment at the classroom level, district assessments might be used to gather data on content knowledge learned, measure student growth, or compare teaching methods to improve instruction within a grade level or school. These are typically more formal than classroom assessments, and given quarterly to measure specific skills or content. These can also be a valuable tool in painting a picture of how students, classrooms, and schools are performing in comparison to others in similar settings.

Standardized, higher stakes tests are of course the hot topic in education right now, and controversy surrounds them. Usually when standardized testing is discussed, people are referring to state mandated testing typically administered once a year in certain grade levels. According to Merriam-Webster's dictionary a standardized test is defined as a test whose reliability has been established by obtaining an average score of a significantly large number of individuals for use as a standard of comparison. A standardized test is given in the same way to all test takers, under the same conditions, and is evaluated in the same way for every group who takes it. This consistency in administering the tests ideally allows for reliable comparison of the results across all test takers.

Standardized tests absolutely play a legitimate role in evaluating students. First of all, a standardized test is more objective than some other forms of evaluation. It is a snapshot in time of a student's knowledge on a particular topic. It does not always evaluate everything a student does know, but can definitely tell you what they don't know. While it is not always a complete picture, it can point out obvious gaps in learning, and when used in combination with other student outcomes on class work, projects, or observations, can help provide a clear picture of a students' progress. This is valuable because it removes subjectivity. Tests are graded by computer or by an independent third party. While I may see a student's work one way (especially with a more subjective piece of work, like writing), another teacher may see things another way.

Standardized tests also give you a simple comparison to the "norm" for other students in similar situations. The questions are tested, and the test norm referenced and research based. Test makers attempt to remove bias and confusion from test questions before the tests are administered. When used as one piece of data in a comprehensive approach to determine how a student is doing in a particular area, standardized tests can be valuable tools.

However, the high stakes nature of these tests is concerning. Student performance on these types of tests is often tied to funding, formal teacher evaluations and pay, and even student promotion to the next grade or graduation. When so many important things are at stake based on the results from one test, problems will arise.

The areas tested start to be the only areas focused on. Typically reading, writing, and math are heavily emphasized, which can leave little room for other important areas of study such as science and social studies, and even less room for the arts. When teachers know their students will be tested only in certain areas, it's tempting to neglect other areas. Districts are even doing away with some subjects all together, because the pressure to use instructional time for tested subjects takes priority. This can lead to an incomplete education for our students.

When teacher evaluations and pay are linked to these types of tests, the worry is that cheating and leading students to correct answers will take place because so much is at stake. It also puts teachers in an unfair position, and makes it difficult to retain good teachers in high need areas. It discourages teachers from serving populations with diverse needs, who may not do as well on these tests, such as special education students, and English language learners.

This is an area which has dramatically changed even in the eight years I've been teaching, and it often leaves teachers frustrated and discouraged. I don't feel good about testing my kids so often that there's no time to teach them. I don't feel good about kindergarteners taking intensive time consuming tests that need to be individually administered. How can that not negatively affect the time spent on instruction and building relationships with students? I also don't have all the answers. I don't know where exactly the balance should be between accountability and teacher autonomy. It is a complex problem, involving policy and politics beyond the scope of this book. I don't have the answers, but I do know we need to start asking more questions about how this new era of high stakes testing is drastically impacting education for our kids.

Keeping Perspective

Grades and tests are not going anywhere, and while there are obvious problems with our current systems, it's unrealistic to think things will change overnight. I think it's important to maintain a sense of perspective and balance, remembering one grade or test score is not the total measure of a student's learning or worth.

So how do we keep things in perspective? How do we encourage our kids to do their best while allowing for mistakes? How do we hold a child accountable for their learning, while supporting them as they learn lessons about responsibility and independence? How do we maintain high but realistic expectations for achievement? Here are a few practical things to keep in mind as your children forge ahead into the land of letter grades and standardized tests:

A grade is a summary. Grades should be summaries of a child's academic achievement and a condensed overview of how they are doing. They are not the whole picture.

A test score is a snapshot. Remember tests give you a quick look into a child's knowledge on a particular topic at one moment in time. It is valuable when used with other assessments, but is limited in showing you only how they performed during that given week, month, assignment or semester.

Communicate. Be open. Talk with your child's teacher about their strengths and weaknesses throughout the entire school year to get a clear, complete picture of their academic progress. Ask questions when things don't seem to make sense.

Everyone needs a success per day. I am a firm believer in high expectations. I run a tight ship in my classroom, and my students tend to progress well. But high expectations need to be realistic expectations, and we need to remember they are kids, balancing challenges that might frustrate them with opportunities for success. This might mean breaking a larger task or assessment into smaller pieces. It may mean backing up and reviewing foundational concepts before moving on to more complex ones. For example, a child may not be capable at this point in time of getting straight A's. But perhaps you could focus on praising him when he gets all his work in on time, a necessary success toward getting better grades. Kids need opportunities to succeed on a regular basis, and need those successes to maintain motivation. While kids need to be challenged, everything can't be a challenge. Nobody, adults included, continue to be motivated without experiencing some measure of success throughout the day. Small successes need to be built upon to create larger ones.

Make your child the standard. The most effective means of assessment and evaluation is to compare a student only to themselves. If a student is making progress, that is what matters. True progress means individual improvement over time toward certain goals, and those goals may be different depending on the child. While we certainly need to keep in mind what is developmentally expected around certain ages, the focus (especially with very young children) needs to be growth, not comparison to other children. In a society where everything from feeding choices to when your child crawls or walks has become a competitive sport, it is no wonder we easily fall into comparing children to other children and setting them up to compete against one another. While some healthy competition is good and even necessary, I think the most important thing to remember when talking about grades and evaluating academic success is to maintain a growth mindset. Only compare your children to themselves, measuring their growth against where they were earlier.

It's ok to be average. We too often rush to label a child as gifted and a genius when they are good at something. On the flip side we immediately want to identify a problem or label if a child is not excelling in a particular area. It's really ok for them to be allowed to develop at an average rate and just be a kid. Don't assume because they haven't mastered something yet, it means they are a bad student, their teacher is a bad teacher, or they are doomed to struggle throughout their academic careers. Sometimes kids just need time, and they'll eventually get it. Allow them to grow and add new skills, and don't panic if they aren't excelling in every single academic area right away.

Focus on the learning. Praise kids more often for what they're learning than the scores they're receiving. When parents pay for grades or build in too many external rewards, the focus can become skewed, and it can put unnecessary external pressure on kids. Talk about the ways they've grown and improved, and what they can do to continue to learn more.

Remember they are not your grades and scores. Advocate for your child, and be informed about testing and grading policies, but resist the temptation to do things for them or take on all the responsibility for their success.

Discourage test anxiety. Children feed off of the energy of adults around them. Never make more out of a test than it is. Help children focus on just doing their personal best. Remind them tests are just a chance to show what they know. Being worried about doing poorly on a test is usually a self-fulfilling prophecy.

Keep the end goal in mind. The goal of education is to produce thoughtful, productive members of society. In the end, the lessons learned about life will be more important than their GPA or SAT score.

Grades and test scores can be important indicators, but they are also only one small part of authentic assessment. Just because adults are concerned with the final result, doesn't mean kids will be. It also doesn't mean those results are the most important part of teaching and learning. Students need to understand ahead of time how they will be evaluated, and evaluations of any kind should be used as tools to inform instruction. They should tell us where students need more work, or and what we can help them with. Assessment should give an indication of where a teacher might need to do some re-teaching or give more support. We should focus on determining what students know, not just what they don't.

In the high stakes educational environment of testing, grades, and data, everyone has more pressure on them to succeed. Kids are no exception. Half day kindergarten is almost a thing of the past as we push for more instructional time, more achievement, and more progress, jamming more in and expecting kids to thrive. Children are being pushed earlier and earlier to strive for excellence. As an adult, you can help them by understanding how they are being evaluated, and the proper role of those evaluations in their overall success. You can remember grades are a summary, tests are a snapshot, and neither is a complete picture of your child's learning or worth.

"True learning and growth cannot be assessed by a single multiple choice question, nor be reduced to a simple letter grade. We must remember that we teach children first and foremost; their progress, advancement and learning are just as complicated as they are. If you want to see the whole picture, you need to step back and move beyond the academic snapshot."

Jennifer Farrlley, K-12 Education Specialist

CHAPTER TWLEVE: *PROJECTS, HOMEWORK, AND WHY WE'RE WASTING OUR TIME*

Most of the stories I've shared have been about my students, but there is one about my own elementary school days that my parents won't let me live down. I was usually a very conscientious student. I loved school, got good grades, and couldn't wait to grow up to be a teacher. But even the most committed scholars have moments when they just aren't feeling it.

One particular night in second grade, I just did not feel like doing my homework. Like almost every other Wednesday night, I had a math worksheet to do. It dawned on me for the first time to intentionally leave the homework in my desk and convince my parents I didn't have any homework that night. I was pleased with my own brilliance, and thought surely I must be the first child in the history of the universe to think of such a clever plan. How could it go wrong? There was no homework in my backpack, so of course they would believe I didn't have any homework.

When my parents asked me to get started on my homework that night, the moment of truth had arrived. My best acting skills were tested.

I first pretended I hadn't heard them, "Wha…?"I asked flipping my hair around as if they'd caught me off guard, and staring at them with my mouth slightly open and eyes wide.

"Your homework," my mom said, "Time to do it."

"Oh, homework," I chuckled. I mumbled something as nonchalantly as possible about not having any with a dismissive wave of my hand and careful avoidance of eye contact.

"Hmmm, that's strange," my dad said, because it's Wednesday, and you always have homework on Wednesdays.

"Dad!" I said getting instantly defensive (the first sign a second grader is lying) "Mrs. Wheeler told us we don't have any today. I swear!"

"Oh really? Why's that?" my dad asked innocently.

Panic. I hadn't counted on him asking so many pesky questions. (That's the other weakness of a second grade lie, it's usually only been thought out to the first obstacle.) I was visibly flustered now, and I knew I had to think of something fast. "Dad! I don't know! I think it's because the homework factory didn't deliver it today," I said in all seriousness.

I knew I was toast, but I actually hoped against all odds that my parents would buy my homework factory story. I should have known it wasn't going well when my mom practically fell off the couch laughing. I was busted, but at least if I was going to lie, I had made it entertaining.

It's a funny little story, but in reality the homework factory is a great picture of how we often treat homework in our education system. In many cases we're still manufacturing assignments, and sending them home like clockwork, whether they're valuable assignments or not. Teacher teaches, students practice, teacher assigns homework on predetermined nights. It is turned in, graded, and tested on, without much thought to the whole process because it's just what we've always done.

It's become like a factory, truly, with dedicated little worker bees (students) turning out their product (the homework). Their supervisors (parents and teachers) are forced to hold them accountable and carefully monitor their production. There's not a lot of thought given to the engagement of the workers in the factory, if they're learning from this method, or what they're doing with that final product. It's just simply homework in, homework complete, homework out. It's more a matter of routine than learning.

The longer I teach, the more I wonder if homework is a good thing. I really don't think we should be assigning it the way we do anymore, and I'm not the only one.

The Homework Myth, by Alfie Kohn challenges the notion that homework is inherently good. His ideas have started an avalanche of teachers, and the general public, questioning the way we do homework and how we define success for our kids. There are many negative aspects of homework for parents, families, teachers, and most importantly, students.

Kids Hate Homework

This certainly comes as no surprise. Kids also hate cleaning their room or eating vegetables. That doesn't necessarily mean those things aren't good for them. But when kids hate something, and it's a battle to get them to do it every night, shouldn't we look at how we're doing it, and how it could be done better? If kids felt the same way about school every day, we would think there was something wrong. While there are certainly aspects of school which can be boring and just need to be done, don't we make attempts at making school relevant and fun? Don't best practices in teaching suggest that kids who like what they're doing and have positive attitudes about school do better? Maybe we should look at homework the same way.

On top of that, the evidence to suggest that homework is even good for kids in the first place is inconclusive at best. Alfred Kohn points out that the evidence, or lack thereof, speaks for itself.

> ". . . the fact is that after decades of research on the topic, there is no overall positive correlation between homework and achievement (by any measure) for students before middle school or, in many cases, before high school. More precisely, there's virtually no good research on the impact of homework in the primary grades – and therefore no data to support its use with young children – whereas research has been done with students in the upper elementary grades, and it generally fails to find any benefit"(Kohn

2006, 37)[1]

Parents Hate Homework

Homework has become an emotionally charged subject, and one that often causes disagreements between parents and teachers. Nothing gets parents riled up faster than homework, but I have to tell you: the reasons they are riled are never the same. Some are upset because there's too much homework, others are upset because there is too little. One mom actually asked me to get some extra work together for her speedy-working son. She had four other little ones at home, and didn't have time to keep him occupied and take care of all of them. She needed something to keep him busy. Um. . . no.

I'm sure as a parent you've felt torn on this particular subject as well. If your kids have too much homework, you worry about them not having time for other activities, or time to play and just be a kid. If they don't have enough homework, you wonder what they're actually learning in school. On top of that, you're not even really sure what is too much or not enough? You talk to other parents about it, but like many other things, how much homework their kids have seems to be a competition.

I would be willing to bet you might hate homework even more than your kids do. It's a draw on precious family time, requires you to play the role of both teacher and police officer to make sure it gets done, and creates a sometimes nightly battlefield complete with blood, sweat, and tears.

Homework is not exactly positive parent involvement. I don't think anyone relishes the hours spent working on homework instead of doing a fun activity or even just reading together as a family. I don't think the nightly struggle to get your kids to do homework makes you feel connected to and involved in their education. Especially the way homework is typically assigned, it's just another thing to check off the already packed family to-do list.

In many ways, we are passing down our addiction to busy-ness and productivity to our kids. Parents brag/complain about how many hours of homework their child had the night before or how late they stayed up doing it after their soccer/ballet/karate etc. We spend lots of time and money on making sure our child has the most ornate book report poster, or rainforest diorama that every existed. It even gets to the point where parents clearly have done most of it for their child to avoid the chance it might not be pretty if he does it himself.

If the only reasons homework is being assigned are to increase parental involvement in their child's education, or because parents are demanding it, those are not good enough reasons in my opinion. The role of parents in any assignment should be evaluated carefully. Who has ever felt involved and bonded with their child over a math worksheet? Even more involved projects, which cannot be completed independently, often just lead to parents running all over town to find a place that sells poster board and glitter paint after 9:00 at night, and then doing way too much of the project themselves.

Teachers Hate Homework

I have another confession for you: Teachers hate homework. We hate putting together the assignments, sending it home, and giving instructions on it. We hate getting ceaseless parent questions about it. We hate that so many parents complain about how much homework we're giving, either too little or too much in their estimation.

It's difficult to find the balance between what children can do mostly independently at home and what will still challenge them. Sometimes teachers just want them to get extra practice with a skill, but there's no guarantee they'll be practicing it correctly at home. Practicing can also easily turn into pointless busy work if the homework is too easy for them.

Almost every morning, I would have an email from a parent asking me to excuse someone's homework being late, because they had a family birthday party to go to and they didn't get a chance to do it. Almost every time, I was both incredulous that they hadn't put school first, and sympathetic, because actually family comes first. I probably would have done the exact same thing, and I wanted my students to have meaningful experiences outside of school.

I have struggled greatly with what I believe about homework. At first it seemed crazy to be giving homework to five and six year olds after a full day at school. Common sense suggested it was already a long day, and they just needed time to be kids and spend time with their families.

Then I thought I found some validity in homework as extra practice or preparation, until I realized they were often practicing things the wrong way, which is just as bad as not practicing at all.

Then I reasoned that at least weekly homework would teach responsibility and prepare them for later grade levels, until I realized those kids who were already responsible were the ones doing it, and those that were irresponsible just simply weren't. . . ever.

In desperation and confusion, I hung onto the fact that at least homework involved parents and was a good way to show them what their kids were learning about, until I realized that parents were either complaining about too little or too much homework, or even doing it for their kids just to get it done.

But then I have questions. How do we take on things like larger projects or reading novels in class, without students doing some of the work at home? What about just sending home unfinished work, to catch up, much like my real world? If it's not shown to build responsibility and character, then what will? How do students prepare for upper grades and college where working at home will be expected?

These questions and others keep us doing homework the way it's always been done, despite what we know about student learning and our intuitive feelings about its worth. Tradition unfortunately plays a big role in this vicious homework cycle. We keep assigning it because everyone expects us to. Students, parents, administrators, and even other teachers expect us to assign homework. Students think they're getting away with something if we don't assign it, or even that they won't do as well on the test/project/ etc. Parents often complain about homework, but the truth of the matter is, they expect it, and mistakenly equate it with academic rigor and challenging their kids. Other teachers don't want anyone to rock the boat. They often want to keep doing things the way they've always been done. They don't want colleagues to stop giving homework, because then they might be expected to stop also. Teachers have built grading systems and teaching methods around homework. Even the course material they can cover (particularly in older grades) depends on students being expected to do a lot of the work or reading at home.

Instead of Homework

I am not suggesting we do away with homework altogether. In fact, I think that if meaningful, engaging learning is going on in our classrooms, it will very naturally spill over into time at home. But I think we need to move away from a homework policy that states we will be having homework, to one that says we won't unless it's important.

Think about this: If teachers just make a policy at the beginning of the year that homework will go home every Monday and is due by that Friday, no matter what, and then later have to come up with what that homework actually is, aren't we admitting the value is really in consistency and a schedule and not the work taking up the children's time?

What if we moved more to a policy that says, unless it is meaningful to continue something at home, we won't. Teachers would think really long and hard before assigning any homework, and the homework that did go home would then be more valuable, and perhaps taken more seriously.

Are we sacrificing real learning for busyness? Is the goal of homework to extend learning or give the illusion of learning? Is quality being substituted for quantity? Are students beginning to resent learning because it is represented to them as a series of irrelevant and tedious tasks?

In my experience, the area of homework is one in which what we know about the way human beings learn and grow does not matching our current practices. Administrators talk about relevance and the importance of standards-based teaching, but then force teachers to come up with a formal homework policy. It even comes down to calculating how long a homework assignment will take a child to complete to make sure it is within the mandated district minutes a child is allowed to spend on homework each night. Reality doesn't match the message, and reality doesn't match the message with our kids either.

Ways to Make Homework Worthwhile

Homework as a mandated general policy needs to be done away with, but I do believe homework has a place in our educational system today. I think if we are teaching kids to extend their learning and apply what they're learning to situations outside of school, then naturally students will spend time on work at home. Projects which ask students to apply a concept they've learned, and which are open-ended, allowing for the option to work on it at home would be worthwhile.

I think it's also ok for there to be an occasional need to catch up on or finish work which wasn't finished at school during time at home. That's an actual, relevant life lesson. If I don't get my work done at school, sometimes I need to take it home to get it done. But, I think if that becomes the rule instead of the exception, we need to examine the amount of time we are giving kids to finish things in school more closely or look into reasons an individual child may be struggling to finish.

My personal opinion is assignments which naturally lend themselves to activities students would do at home anyway like reading, or give families choices of activities to do, are much more worthwhile. Plus I just think families should be the ones deciding how evenings are spent, not schools. Students are already with schools the majority of the day. They need family time and room for other activities.

Most teachers do their best to work within school and

district homework policies and make homework as meaningful as possible. While homework has a long way to come, and there are definitely some improvements which need to be made, I think it is safe to say it will still be a fact of life in households across the country for a while. So I wanted to give you some tips to avoid the battle and make the most out of homework in the meantime:

Establish a routine. If your child has to do homework, establishing an organized time and place to do it helps to alleviate some of the stress and makes the expectations for homework time clear. Avoid spending unnecessary time clearing a spot on the table to do the work or hunting for a writing utensil.

Let them do it. Establish routines together, check in on them, and help them when needed, but remember it's their homework. Never do it for them just to get it done. Even if the assignment is less than great in your opinion, doing it for them sends a bad message. Make it clear they are responsible for their own learning and turning things in on time. You can always talk to the teacher about concerns later on.

Don't hover. In my experience as a teacher, sometimes adults hover over the children who we think will not do their work otherwise. In fact those very children often need the space the most. They might be insecure about doing things the wrong way, so they do nothing, or they have not yet learned to work independently. By sitting right on top of them, watching their every move, adults reinforce the habit of not working unless someone is directly watching them. Try this instead—tell them to do the next two problems and come show you when they're finished. Then walk away. They won't feel constantly watched and insecure, and you'll send the message that their work is their responsibility, and you expect them to do it. If we're always there, they won't learn to work without us.

Communicate with their teacher. If an assignment seems to be taking an unreasonable amount of time or is too difficult, kindly let the teacher know. Admittedly, sometimes an activity just doesn't work out like we'd planned as teachers. In the classroom this is easy to see and correct, but when it's homework we need you to let us know how it's going. It is possible the teacher didn't realize how long it would take, and kindly letting her know could prevent her from sending something like that home in the future. Communicate particular areas you see your child struggling with, too. You sometimes get a better look at how your child is doing with a concept than we get with 30 kids in the room.

Don't be a perfectionist. If your child is doing their personal best, let that be good enough. Resist the urge to overcorrect them or make everything perfect. Also fight the urge to make the biggest, baddest book report poster or science project. If your child would not be able to do it without your assistance (other than purchasing materials), then it probably is going to be you doing most of the work.

Make a plan. If your child has a particularly heavy homework night, help them plan out how they're going to tackle it and break it into smaller chunks. Sometimes it seems overwhelming to kids who haven't learned some of those organizational skills yet, so your role would be to help them make a plan of action.

Ask questions. When offering help on homework, challenge yourself to ask as many questions as possible. Questions keep your child thinking and guide them without doing it for them. For example if they are having a hard time getting started ask, "Where can you begin?" or "What do the directions say?" While they're working you could ask things like, "What do you need to do next?" or "Where could you look to help you with that?" When they're finished with a task ask them, "How did you get that answer?" or "Could you explain that to me?" Asking questions is also a great way for children to reinforce what they've learned.

Be positive. Show a genuine interest in what they're doing and find ways to make it fun and relevant. Our enthusiasm and attitude as adults can greatly shape our kid's attitudes toward homework. Praise them for a job well done, and encourage them when they're frustrated. Phrases like, "You should know how to do this," or "Why is this so hard for you?" are not very helpful and just add to the frustration.

Know your child's limits. You are the parent. If your child has had an exceptionally long or difficult day, make the call to send them to bed or have some downtime instead of doing their homework. You can always wake them up earlier in the morning to get it done if it's becoming a major battle that night. Sometimes a good night's rest or a mental break is all we need, and kids don't always know how to take one themselves.

The best homework is time with you. Kids don't need to be busy all the time. Don't assume lots of homework equals lots of learning. Having dinner together, playing outside, or just snuggling up on the couch and watching a movie with you are some of the best things you can do with your child. They need you more than they need to keep busy.

Just like anything else in the classroom, the more say and

CANDID CLASSROOM

involvement students have in making their own learning choices, the more valuable the learning experience. Therefore, students should have input into whether or not something even needs to be done at home. If they can use their time wisely and get it done at school, isn't that a valuable skill to learn? If they can choose what book they will read or what topic they will research given a set of parameters, aren't they likely to want to do it at home instead of engaging in a nightly homework battle?

> "Teachers' choices about homework are often limited, because many districts mandate homework. But, good teachers put a lot of thought, time, and energy into making homework fun and relevant and appreciate the effort parents put into their child's learning at home.
>
> ***Julia Brink, First Grade Teacher***

207

CHAPTER THIRTEEN: *CHEERIOS, LIFE LESSONS, AND HOW TEACHERS ARE STUDENTS TOO*

It was morning snack time in my kindergarten class, and I often pulled up a tiny chair and joined my students at their tables with a snack of my own. It gave me a chance to build relationships with my students and practice conversation skills with them. This particular day, my snack of choice was some Multigrain Cheerios I had hastily thrown into a baggie on the way out the door. I happily nibbled away on the lightly sweetened little O's as I listened to my kids talk about their pretzels and juice.

After snack, we moved to the carpet for a writing lesson at the easel. I was opening up the lesson with a riveting explanation of the difference between writing a b and a d when Nadia, my very bright, very polite student shot her hand up in the air.

"Not now Nadia," I calmly dismissed her. "You can ask your question when I'm done talking."

"But. . . I see something. . . a Cheerio," she uncharacteristically insisted.

"Ok, but we're not talking about that right now," I replied, turning back to my easel and continuing on with the lesson. After I dismissed them to their tables to practice writing their b's and d's, Natalie came up to me privately.

"Mrs. Ladd?" she began shyly.

"Yes Nadia. What is it?" I responded.

"Well, the Cheerio I saw…it's on your butt."

Horrified, I looked behind me, and sure enough, there was one of my beloved Multigrain Cheerios sticking to my backside. I had been teaching with it stuck to me the entire time, and that is what she had been trying to tell me. I had arrogantly carried on with my lesson, as if anybody cared about b's and d's with an 'o' stuck to my rear end.

That day Nadia reminded me to listen before I talk, and that no matter how much I think I know, I can always learn something from everybody I come across. Teachers are used to teaching. We are used to disseminating our knowledge to the masses. We admittedly make some of the worst students. Trying to run a meeting or workshop for teachers is horrible. Everyone talks at the same time, raises their hands to argue your point, or just doesn't pay attention because we're grading papers from earlier in the day.

But the longer I teach the more I realize I have to learn, and I am so grateful to the students, parents, and other teachers who have taught me so much.

Student Teachers

There are two years of my teaching experience in particular that stick out for me. One stands out because it was one of my best years, the other because it was one of my hardest, but both because I learned so much from my students.

That first year teaching was one of my most memorable. They say you never forget your first class. At the time I had my dream job, a classroom of 17 English Language Learners in a Sheltered English Immersion kindergarten program. All my students were learning English as their second language, while simultaneously learning the regular concepts of kindergarten. I had the sweetest, most adorable class of kids, but could not believe how hard this job was, how overwhelmed I felt.

That group of children has had the most profound impact on me. Getting my own classroom for the first time and hearing them call me 'Maestra' was such an honor. Unexpected little rewards from being a teacher popped up everywhere. I was exhausted and never could have imagined how much work went into this profession I had chosen, but they made me feel creative, and needed, and alive.

That was the sappy version of my first year teaching. The more down to earth version acknowledges how hard it really was. I was working on finishing my license while teaching for the first time. I don't recommend it. The good part was I basically did on-the-job student teaching, instead of the kind of student teaching where you don't get paid. (You do know that right? Teachers work for six months at the end of their college experience, full time, without getting paid? Many don't know that.) It was killer to be a full-time student and a full-time teacher in the same year. God must have felt pity for me though when He blessed me with the sweetest, quirkiest little bunch of kiddos who made getting out of bed every morning possible when everything in me was screaming to lay back down.

I came across a list I thought I had lost the other day, in my journal from my first year teaching. I had written it on the last day of school, feeling nostalgic and wanting to document that crazy first year. I had made it a point to write it the last afternoon of that school year, while my students were playing with all their favorite games and puzzles one last time before summer vacation. I was emotional and missing them already, so I decided to sit and write down what each of them had taught me.

As my eyes filled with tears, I intentionally looked at each one of them and thought about the most important thing I had learned from that student. About an hour later, I would walk them out the door, hug them goodbye one last time, and proceed to ugly cry all the way back to my empty classroom. I will never forget that first group of kiddos and all they taught me about teaching and life.

Namar taught me that patience and neatness really are virtues worth aspiring to. Estaban taught me that sometimes people just need to be heard. Lucia taught me that confidence is the difference between can and can't. Alonso taught me everyone needs someone who expects something from them. Camila taught me that charm combined with intelligence goes a long way. Andrea taught me a lot can be accomplished in nine months. Francisco taught me I have a lot to learn. Theo taught me that a quick wit is not just an adult trait. Jesus taught me that great families come in all shapes and sizes, and are the most important thing. Eddie taught me life can be short and fragile. Emilio taught me the human mind is a fascinating, imaginative place. Ricky taught me a lot is often going on behind a quiet smile. Martina taught me everyone needs somebody to be proud of them. Omar taught me that great ideas often start with dimples and raised eyebrows. Sophia taught me that a sweet spirit is the same in any language. Mia taught me people need support to try new things. Ahkam taught me that children are far more resilient than I am.

I'm disappointed I didn't make that kind of list every year. The new shininess wears off a bit after the first year teaching. Disillusionment and exhaustion set in, and quite frankly, there are certain groups of kids who you are not quite as sad to see move on. Still, I wish I would have kept up the habit on that last day of school because the tough school years, especially the tough ones, taught me the most.

One of those tough years in which I learned so much from my students, was a year teaching out of my comfort zone. When I first moved from Wisconsin to Arizona, I took a job as a special education teacher. They had a huge need, and I really wanted to move. So I took the job opening, telling myself I'd give it a try. I was emergency certified in special ed. for that year, and decided if I ended up loving it, I would go back for my special education license.

Well, I didn't love it. In fact, I hated a lot about it. I missed having my own classroom full of kids all day. I missed being the main teacher, and cultivating a community with the same group of kids all day. The paperwork and legal aspect of the job were overwhelming. The kids were wonderful, but I just didn't feel like I was making adequate progress with them.

It was one of the toughest years I've ever had, but in spite of that, I learned so much. If my first year teaching was me in my element, this year was definitely me out of my element. At the end of that school year, I did make a list before going back to regular education, of the top ten things I learned from teaching special education for a year.

Document, document, document.

Assignments can be modified beyond what I thought possible.

Without student motivation, it doesn't matter how you've modified said assignment.

The key is always finding out what makes a student tick.

A sense of humor is invaluable.

One cannot underestimate the importance of a good educational assistant/classroom aide.

Sometimes students don't get what is best for them because of things out of your control, so in those cases my best within the situation has to be good enough.

Teacher collaboration and planning is becoming more and more essential. (This is hard for me as I considered myself bossy and a smidge controlling when it comes to the classroom. I learned A LOT about this and am really glad I did.)

Kids need to feel successful at something every day.

A parent's love for their child is a powerful force.

I can handle more than I thought I could!

Teachers Teaching Teachers

My fellow teachers have also had a profound impact on me. For the most part, gone are the days when a teacher just closes her classroom door and goes about her merry way, teaching her students in any way she sees fit. Collaboration is necessary and even mandatory in this data-driven age of Professional Learning Communities, and intensive teacher evaluation processes. It can be a challenge to get people who usually call the shots and boss little people around all day, to cooperate and play well with other adults.

My fellow teachers made me a better teacher. I learned about the importance of keeping my voice calm, and finding the fun in the classroom. I learned how to help a struggling student, and make meaningful connections with parents. Vicki and others taught me everything, from how to navigate the political waters of education, to the best way to hang things on the wall in any given building (If I'm ever in charge of designing classrooms, there will be lots of cabinetry and cork board involved. Just saying.) The positive role models I had all around me those first few years of teaching shaped me as a person and a professional in profound ways.

Sometimes other teachers taught me how not to be. I knew I needed to take a break from full-time teaching to pursue writing for a bit, because I didn't want to turn into some of the teachers I had worked with. I told myself that if I was exhausted and burnt out, I would take a break. It's a hard enough job when you love it. It becomes nearly impossible when you don't. I was not ever surprised by the amount of money I made, and in my estimation you can't pay me enough for the valuable job that I do, so I wouldn't even know what to charge. But unfortunately, I watched some fellow teachers care more about what their job wasn't or shouldn't be, than what it was. I saw the exhaustion take a toll and learned from those teachers to take care of myself and be mindful of how I was doing.

I saw teachers who were unwilling to grow or try anything new. They kept recycling the same tired, outdated lessons year after year. There is definitely value in repeating things that work, and having a system in place. There's no need to reinvent the wheel, and I think younger teachers could learn so much from more experienced teachers. But when those experienced teachers are no longer willing to learn from anyone else, let alone teach others, it's time to be done.

Powerful Bonds in the Trenches

Besides all that I learned from my colleagues those first few years teaching, I met one of my dearest friends. She was hired as a transfer from another school a few weeks after school had started. Because our numbers were too high in kindergarten, we needed to open up another class. So we were both the new girls on the kindergarten team, and hit it off instantly.

She had been teaching longer than I had, but her previous school was run much differently than this one. We were both feeling a little lost. We bonded over our mutual admission that we didn't have the foggiest clue what we were doing. It would start off by one of us coming to the other's classroom to ask each other a silly question first before going to a more experienced member of the team and risking looking foolish. Those conversations turned into closing the door and slumping into a chair, admitting that we had no clue what we were doing, and often eating Tootsie Rolls leftover from the Halloween party by the handful.

Eventually our afterschool gripe sessions turned into talking about life and dreams, and our mutual passion for teaching and developed into a strong friendship. We live across the country from each other now, but since those days teaching together, we've shared so much of life together. I've had the privilege of standing up in her wedding to marry a great guy. I just got a text message

from him this morning that they've had their first baby. This Auntie Ladd can't wait to meet him and spoil him. Powerful bonds are formed in the trenches of education—over Tootsie Rolls, on tiny chairs after the students go home.

We Learn From You

Parent teacher conferences were some of the most stressful, but best parts of my job. Twice a year, around conference time, I would get myself all worked up. It was a busy time of year, and it made for long days of staying at school until well into the evening. It made me nervous to meet with all those parents at first, and I was afraid they'd tell me they were unhappy with the job I was doing or the school. But then, every year without fail, I would walk away from parent teacher conferences with a new appreciation for my students and a renewed commitment to my job.

Something always stuck with me from those meetings with parents, and it was never how long the night had been. It was the intense love you have for your children. Seeing your kids through your eyes always changed my perspective and renewed my commitment to them. Hearing your stories about them playing with their siblings, or about visiting their grandparents made me remember they are little and innocent. Seeing your eyes light up when I told you how well they were doing, or that they really had made a lot of progress, gave me the motivation I needed to keep working hard to make sure they kept making that progress. I would go home after conferences every single time and talk my husband's ear off, telling him about all the wonderful parents I had met, and how differently I looked at their kids as a result.

As teachers and parents we may have our differences, and unfortunately the current political battlefield of education often pits teachers and schools against the communities and families they serve. But I want you to know you inspire me. Your love and dedication to your children is breathtaking, and your hard work with them does not go unnoticed. I want you to know you matter to your kids, and you're doing a good job. I want you to know I see how difficult it is to send them off into the world, and I am honored you trust me with them five days a week. Most of all, I want you to know we're on the same team, and you are the most valuable player.

"One of the greatest outcomes of being an educator is the relationships we build with our students, their families, and our fellow educators."

Christine Geyer, Assistant Principal

NOTES

Chapter 2: Helicopters, Independence, and Why You Should Stop Carrying Your Child's Backpack

1) Postal, Karen Spangenberg. 2011. "How Structure Improves Your Child's Brain: Teaching Self-Regulation Without Overstepping Your Bounds." Psychology Today. November 11.

2) Thompson, Dr. Michael. 2012. Homesick and Happy: How Time Away from Parents Can Help a Child Grow. New York. Ballantine Books

Chapter 4: Recess, Social Skills, and the Truth about Bullying

1) Melton, Glennon Doyle. 2013. Carry On, Warrior: Thoughts On Life Unarmed. New York: Scribner.

2) Porter, Susan Eva. 2013. Bully Nation: Why America's Approach to Childhood Aggression is Bad for Everyone. Saint Paul: Paragon House.

Chapter 8: Spelling, Changes, and What Happened to Cursive

1) Gladstone, Karen. 2010. "Handwriting Matters; Cursive Doesn't." New York Times, April 30.

http://www.nytimes.com/roomfordebate/2013/
04/30/should-schools-require-children-to-learn-
cursive/handwriting-matters-cursive-doesnt.

Chapter 9: Reading, Writing, and How to Raise Kids Who Do Both

1)Mem Fox. 2013. "Ten Read-aloud
Commandments." Accessed January 24.
http://memfox.com/forparents/for-parents-ten-
read-aloud-commandments/.

Chapter 10: Cards, Dice, and Why Everyone Can Do Math

1) Bornstein, David. 2011. "A Better Way to
Teach Math." New York Times, April 18.
Accessed January 24, 2014.
http://opinionator.blogs.nytimes.com/2011/04/
18/a-better-way-to-teach-math/?_r=1

Chapter 12: Projects, Practice, and Why Teachers Hate Homework

1)Kohn, Alfred. 2006. The Homework Myth: Why
Our Kids Get Too Much of a Bad Thing.
Cambridge: De Capo Press.

THANK YOU

Thank you to my students, all of you over the years. I am so proud to have been your teacher, and you have taught me more than you know. Thank you to the parents of those students, who trusted me with your most precious gifts, and allowed me the extraordinary privilege of helping you educate your children.

Thank you to my fellow educators. You truly do have one of the hardest jobs in the world, and you do it with such dedication and determination. You inspire me, and I hope I've done you justice in this book. A special thanks to those of you who took time out of your busy schedules to lend me your perspective and your words: Jill Traxler, Amy Denny, Jenny Harmon, Erik Kamrath, Vicki Sharkey, Heidi Evans, Amber Clark, Jessica Kamrath, Lynda Patterson, Brigid Johannes, Tara Dunn, Matt Rawley, Aubrey Ruhser, Stacey Noel, Vicki Foley, Brian Butson, Jennifer Farrlley, Julia Brink, and Christine Geyer.

Thank you to my very favorite author, Shauna Niequist. Reading your books allowed me to see myself as a writer. Thank you for your honesty. Thank you for telling the truth about things that matter. Thank you, most of all, for your tweet about Prodigal

Press, which led me to this incredible opportunity.

Thank you to those who actually made this book happen. Thanks to Christy McFaren, for the beautiful cover design, Ben Arment, for the coaching and insight, Stephanie for the editing help, and Darrell Vesterfelt, for printing logistics. Most of all, thank you Darrell and Allison Vesterfelt, for sharing your invaluable expertise and guidance. Thank you for seeing something in my idea, and giving me the tools to make it a reality. Thank you for your intense passion for helping people live better stories, and thank you for partnering with me to tell mine.

Thank you to my encouraging friends for your excitement and support. A special thanks to my next door neighbor and creative partner in crime, Kelsey Wharton. Thank you for reading awful first drafts, and keeping me on track. Creative Club forever!

Thank you to my family. Thanks Mom and Dad, for always encouraging me to tell my stories, and Grandma for soaking up every one of them. To some of my favorite people on the planet— my siblings, David, Emily, Kelli, Ben, and Jess—your support means everything to me, and your creativity and passion inspire me daily. To all my nieces, thank you for the privilege of watching you grow from another perspective. Thank you, Emma, Anahi, and Paige, for inspiring this book when you started kindergarten.

Finally my deepest gratitude to my dear Mr. Ladd, who told me I didn't need an excuse to follow my dream.

CPSIA information can be obtained
at www.ICGtesting.com
Printed in the USA
LVHW05s1736230818
587903LV00013B/1448/P